This Is My Beloved Son

Jesus, the Man

This Is My Beloved Son

Jesus, the Man

Matthew 3:16, 17

by
The Rev. Doyle Herbert Snyder

CCB Publishing
British Columbia, Canada

This Is My Beloved Son:
Jesus, the Man

Copyright ©2014 by Beverly Franks Snyder
ISBN-13   978-1-77143-181-1
First Edition

Library and Archives Canada Cataloguing in Publication
Snyder, Doyle Herbert, 1927-2014, author
This is my beloved son : Jesus, the man / by Doyle Herbert Snyder. -- First Edition.
Issued in print and electronic formats.
ISBN 978-1-77143-181-1 (pbk.).--ISBN 978-1-77143-182-8 (pdf)
Additional cataloguing data available from Library and Archives Canada

Thanks to the Rev. John W. Sloat for the number of hours he spent making this book a possibility. Also, grateful thanks to Waltraud "Wally" Hendel for the beautiful painting of Jesus used on the cover of this book.

Publisher: CCB Publishing
                British Columbia, Canada
                www.ccbpublishing.com

Dedication

This book is
respectfully and lovingly
dedicated to the memory of

Doyle Herbert Snyder
1927-2014

by his wife of 60 years
Beverly Jane Franks Snyder

and the other members of his family:

Melinda Ann Snyder and Rik Mangino
Katherine, Daniel, Michael, Kevin

Rebecca Jane Snyder and Hugh Graham
Christopher, Hannah, Brittany, Dmitry

Suzanne Noel Snyder and Rich Paukovics
Julia, Bergen, Jason

Rachel Elizabeth Snyder Mackintosh

Great-grandchildren
Eden Elizabeth Graham, Penelope Kate Lee

About The Author

Doyle Herbert Snyder was born in Uniontown, PA, the son of Lena Maude Browning and Carl Dewey Snyder. He was raised in the Chestnut Ridge Mountains in a home built by his father. He attended a one-room schoolhouse and was a lifelong seeker of the truth.

He was grateful to the American Sunday School Union and John Strabel of Scottdale for his knowledge of and devotion to the Scriptures.

Doyle's father and others in the area founded and built the W. F. Union Chapel which Doyle attended through high school and college. He joined the Navy and became a member of the Blue Jackets Choir with which he sang on CBS Radio every Sunday morning.

He was attending Waynesburg University, majoring in history, when he met his wife, Beverly Franks. She was a Presbyterian whose grandparents on her mother's side belonged to the Cumberland Presbyterian denomination, and on her father's side founded the first Lutheran Church west of the Allegheny Mountains in 1774.

Upon graduating from college, Doyle enrolled at Western Theological Seminary where he pursued a Bachelor of Theology degree, after which he went on to finish at Pittsburgh Theological Seminary when the two merged. During his second year of seminary, he became student pastor to the Middle Presbyterian Church, Mt. Pleasant, PA, founded in 1773, where he was ordained to the Presbyterian ministry in 1957.

He became pastor to three other churches in western Pennsylvania: the Calvary Presbyterian Church of Donora, the First Presbyterian Church of Monongahela, and the Fremont Ave. Presbyterian Church in Bellevue, which later became Northminster Presbyterian Church after the merger of three Presbyterian congregations.

Doyle was an interim pastor to seven churches in the Pittsburgh, PA area and two in the Cincinnati, OH area. He did not retire until he and his wife moved into the Passavant Retirement Community in Zelienople, PA in 2009, where he died on February 6, 2014.

Tributes

I will show you what someone is like who comes
to me, hears my words and acts on them.
Luke 6:47

"Blessed are the merciful, for they will be shown mercy. Blessed are the pure in heart, for they will see God. Blessed are the peacemakers, for they will be called children of God." Matthew 5:7-9

My grandfather, Doyle Snyder, lived these beatitudes with both grace and adventure. He was first and foremost a Christ follower and after that, to me, a brilliant mix of gentleness and excitement. He did everything he could to invest in his grandchildren and I was a lucky beneficiary of his perseverance.

Some of the very best memories of my life involve my Grandpa. From building play houses and ships, to bible studies in the Rocky Mountains, he had a way of taking his faith and bringing it down into the sawdust and the stones. Give the man some bungee cords and duct tape and he could fix anything, and teach you a lesson in the project. He showed us what it meant to be Christian, not just when it was easy but when we'd been stuck in a car for eight hours fighting with our cousins. His faith and simplicity helped to plant my faith and I only pray that God gives me the grace to be a man like my grandfather.

My Grandpa had four daughters and all the joys and struggles that that brings. As my wife and I sat in the hospital room and were told that we would be expecting our second girl, I knew that Grandpa was smiling. I know that I'll have his prayers from Heaven and know by God's grace I'll see him again in the blessedness of the beatific vision. We probably won't need it, but I'll bring some duct tape.

Christopher Graham

Doyle was such an important part of our lives! We will miss his friendly smile, his kind words, his good advice born of sound judgment, his wisdom in all matters, and his unfaltering faith. He left his mark on so many people – his spirit lives on.

George and Carolyn Pearsall

I first had the privilege of meeting Doyle in 2009 when he and Bev moved to Lutheran Senior Life Passavant Community. Over the years I came to know Doyle as a true gentleman with a sweet spirit. He loved the Lord and his relationship with his Savior was lived out in tangible ways – a sweet smile or a word of encouragement. He loved his family deeply and proudly sang their praises. My life is better for having had the privilege of knowing him, and I trust that as you read his book, yours will be as well.

Laura Roy, CEO
Lutheran Senior Life
Passavant Community

Doyle had a life-long interest and fascination with the person of Jesus of Nazareth. His library reflected this keen interest. Doyle's book is highly readable for the first-time reader who simply wants to know more about Jesus' life, but also for the serious and thoughtful reader who wants to go deeper. To read Doyle's words is to really hear him speaking to us again…I can hear his voice, listen to him shaping his thoughts, drawing conclusions. He writes well and clearly just as he did when he spoke.

Rev. Dr. David and Judy Antonson

I knew Doyle for only a few months before his death, but his striking physical presence and warm spirit made me want to know him better. I had that opportunity when I was privileged to read his book manuscript. What struck me immediately is his unusual skill in combining both traditional faith and objective reasoning. His deep personal faith does not keep him from a critical analysis of scripture: he is not afraid to point out that certain things probably did not happen or that certain other events were metaphors and not literal happenings. This objectivity makes it possible to take even more seriously the conclusions at which he arrives. I think that *This Is My Beloved Son* is a valuable addition to the literature about the life of Jesus of Nazareth.

Rev. John W. Sloat

Doyle served our small country church as a student pastor and became ordained there in 1957. His enthusiasm to do God's work led us into new Christian projects. We had a Bible School. We did evangelical calling in the neighborhood. We built an addition on to the church, the first and only since 1772. Our church grew in many ways with God's help and Doyle's leadership. As a member of his first church, I was happy to have shared in his early ministry.

Mary Elizabeth Hauser

The Rev. Doyle Snyder came to our church as a young minister with his gracious wife Beverly and their energetic children. He was a breath of fresh air for our congregation as we were accustomed to older, more sedate ministers. In his sermons, Doyle tackled issues as far-ranging as poor congregational singing and the civil rights movement of the 1960's. Always inspiring, he spoke with a firm biblical foundation that helped guide us in our everyday lives. C. S. Lewis described friendship as "a glorious likeness to heaven itself, where we will enjoy the presence of God that much more because we will share that special experience with others."

The Rev. Doyle Snyder was a true friend, a wonderful family man, a great intellect who now is surely in the loving arms of "The Beloved Son" enjoying Christian friendship with those who have gone on.

Mary Janet Henry

Contents

Chapter 1

FOUR OBJECTIVES

The first objective is on the life, ministry and teaching of the Jesus his disciples knew and loved, before he was crucified. Of all the things that happened in Jesus' life, his crucifixion has drawn by far the greatest attention, next to his resurrection. It raised questions in the minds of the early Christians with regard both to the sinfulness of humanity and the goodness of God. How could humans possibly inflict such gruesome pain and humiliation on another human? But equally difficult is the question: "How could a just and compassionate God allow such an atrocity to happen to anyone, especially someone as good as Jesus?" The point of this paragraph is that Christians have allowed the life and teaching of Jesus to be overshadowed, and in many ways set aside, by the horror of the crucifixion and the hope of the resurrection. By focusing on his death and resurrection we have found the easy way to get to Heaven when we die; all we have to do is believe and nothing more. But is that what Jesus wanted? In sermons and in worship, do we emphasize the message Jesus addressed to the crowds which came to hear him? Why would he say, *"Take my yoke upon you and learn from me,"* (Matt 11:29 RSV), if he did not think it was important to know his message? Even more to the point are his words in Luke's Gospel: *"Why do you call me, 'Lord, Lord,' but do not do what I tell you?"* (Luke 6:46 RSV). Some say Jesus' teaching cannot save. Even if that were true, his message delivered before the crucifixion should prepare us to be Christian in this life and enable us to live well in the life to come. By focusing on the Jesus the disciples knew and loved, we rediscover essential truths which too often have not received the attention and devotion they deserve.

The second goal is to take the humanity of Jesus with all seriousness, rather than jumping prematurely to his deity. What did his first disciples and followers believe about him and how did it affect them? They could clearly see that Jesus was as human as they were; he got tired, excited, angry, but just as often joyful. He needed nourishment from food every day and at times seemed to need their presence and support. As a result of their exposure to his obvious humanity, they would have rejected the claim that he was the unique Son of God or God in human flesh, which they embraced only after the resurrection, not before. Although they knew he shared their humanity, they were strongly attracted to him because of his magnetic personality, contagious joy, and because he expressed his "good news" with amazing confidence and authority. While the Gospels show they never fully understood his message, they were sure he possessed ultimate answers for the pressing issues facing their people and he promised a new vision of how things could be. The disciples had to be impressed with Jesus' amazing brilliance in expressing his thinking about the ordinary and the extraordinary, the spiritual and the mundane. Few people with maximum training in public speaking could even begin to match his eloquence. The disciples quickly learned to admire and love him.

The third objective is to see how Jesus' message and ministry grew directly out of his personal relationship with God. He loved God whom he referred to as "Abba Father." "Abba" was probably the first word a small child used in addressing his or her father, although other scholars are sure it was simply a substitute for "father." His compassion for the sick, outcasts, sinners, tax collectors and prostitutes, reflected what he learned from the Abba God. He knew from experience that God was full of grace and love, who accepted his children the way they were, with no preconditions. To Jesus, God would never say: "When you change your ways and measure up to my standards, then I will accept you and love you." The proof that Jesus felt this way about God is in the indisputable fact that he daily spent time with people whom the religious elite looked down on and despised, the tax collectors, outcasts and sinners. Jesus accepted these people the way they were, because he was sure that is how God accepts all his children. Jesus did not condemn the outcasts and sinners. He was compassionate toward human weaknesses. Jesus himself did not live a strict life, like John the Baptist. He enjoyed life – a little too much for some of his adversaries. While John preached judgment soon to come, Jesus' message was "God loves you, for God loves sinners." Jesus never devised a program whereby the tax collectors and prostitutes could adopt a more acceptable livelihood. Neither did he demand that they make the appropriate sacrifices in the temple to get right with God. He did say that the tax collectors and sinners would get into the kingdom of God ahead of the self-righteous ones who were sure they understood God's requirements and were fulfilling them all.

The disciples observed Jesus' personal experience of God in his many times of prayer, often alone and at night. This enabled them to see that his message was not his alone, but one which grew out of his remarkable experience of the living God. To his disciples and followers he was an outstanding human being, but his close relationship with God, set him apart from others. This led them to willingly make many sacrifices in order to follow him. It also led them, some time after the resurrection, to conclude that Jesus was the unique Son of God. But this belief did not arise among them before the crucifixion and resurrection. At Caesarea Philippi, Peter declared Jesus to be the Messiah, but that is not the same as designating Jesus as deity.

The fourth objective is to accept the work of dedicated Bible scholars and historians, especially those of the last one hundred years. Their work enables us to know much better the Jesus who truly lived and who was known and loved by the disciples. With all the advances made in every field of learning, it is surprising how many Christians are still afraid to ask questions about the faith and the Bible. This was the obstacle which Jesus faced in his ministry, the ingrained difficulty most of his hearers had in taking a fresh look at their conclusions and practices concerning religion and life.

Because his God-inspired "good news" called for changes in religious and social practices, including the way the Jerusalem Temple was operated, Jesus was ultimately condemned.

To get a better understanding of the Jesus who lived before the crucifixion, it is necessary to take a fresh look at the Bible, cherished by millions as the most helpful book ever written. The Bible enables us see that a power was at work in the past, the same power which caused the "big bang" when the universe began and which has guided the formation of an awesome number of galaxies, moving from one another at an increasing speed, in the limitless expanse of space. Scripture progressively reveals that this power is not all fire and force, but rather is compassionate toward living creatures, a power which feels and yearns and loves, and desires above all to lead its creation to fulfillment in everlasting joy. This power is not power in the usual sense, for its clearest manifestation is in every baby, and certainly in Mary's tiny baby, in whose life and ministry is found the true heart of the living God. We will pursue this wonderful truth in the pages which follow.

Chapter 2

AMAZING SURPRISES

Let us consider some amazing surprises growing out of the life of *"Jesus of Nazareth, the son of Joseph." (John 1:45).*

A little less than 2000 years ago, Jesus was crucified outside Jerusalem. We are not sure of the date of his death. We are not sure of the date of his birth. And yet for succeeding centuries most of the world dated current and past events by this man's assumed birth and millions date their hope of eternal life by this man's death and resurrection.

He may have been only about 33 years old when the Romans ended his life with characteristic brutality. His ministry may have lasted only 12 to 15 months before it was cruelly snuffed out. To the Romans and the High Priest group who wanted him silenced, he was a mere peasant, a nobody, who was not worth a second thought. And yet, as you read this sentence, a million prayers will have been offered to God in his name and an unknown number of devoted scholars are at this very moment studying his life and writing books about him.

While it appears most of the crowds which assembled wherever Jesus traveled came for healing or to witness a healing, many came to hear him talk eloquently and convincingly about the love of God for all people. But he shocked his listeners when he told them they must love their enemies, which certainly included the Romans. And yet the Romans later took delight in abusing and torturing him. Then they stripped him naked and nailed his lacerated body to a cross and let him hang there until he died. But as you read this, someone, somewhere is singing a hymn with words like these: "More love to thee, O Christ, more love to thee!

Hear now the prayer I make on bended knee. This is my earnest plea: More love, O Christ to thee, more love to thee."

Although the relationship with God was so close, God did not remove the cup of suffering and death. And where was the God who hears the desperate cries of his suffering children when Jesus called out from the cross, *"My God, my God, why have you forsaken me?"* How truly human he was when he shared the same spiritual dilemmas that we face. For how often have we prayed for a terminally ill child or parent or friend, but in the end had to let them go when our prayers were not answered and we may have felt they were not even heard? And yet, after some time had passed, we may have discovered we were not alone in our grief, for God was present with us, and had even suffered along with us, as God suffered with Jesus when he died. That is the cost of love, and *"God is love."* (I John 4:8 RSV). In Jesus is the offer of a faith which works in the bright peaks but also in the dark valleys of human experience.

His disciples offer another surprise. Jesus needed them to be with him and to learn from him, but we are frequently told they failed to understand him. And yet, your Christian faith and mine rests on their shoulders. There could be no Christianity without them, frail as they were. But if Jesus had selected men of exceptional gifts, it would not have connected with the people he was most interested in. The disciples needed to be closer to where most people were.

Jesus' relationship with his family provides yet another challenge. According to the gospel of Mark, at least once, his mother, brothers and sisters came to take him home because, they said, *"He is out of his mind."* (Mark 3:21). Mark also says: *"A crowd was sitting around him, and they told him, 'Your mother and brothers are outside looking for you.' 'Who are my mother and my brothers?' he asked. Then he looked at those seated in a circle around him and said, 'Here are my mother and brothers! Whoever does God's will is my brother and sister and mother.'"* (Mark 3:32-35)

John's gospel says his brothers did not believe in him when he took the last journey from Galilee to Jerusalem, when he was apparently convinced that death was unavoidable. His brothers said to him, "*'You ought to leave here and go to Judea, so that your disciples may see the miracles you do. No one who wants to become a public figure acts in secret. Since you are doing these things, show yourself to the world.' For even his own brothers did not believe in him.*" (John 7:3-5).). And yet, his mother was present near the cross when he died, and following his death and resurrection, his family did believe in him and his brother, James, eventually became the leader of the Jerusalem church.

Some scholars are convinced that Jesus' family always believed in his work, but disagreed in the way he carried it out. They may have wanted Jesus to settle down in Nazareth and let people come to him for healing, which would have greatly increased the position and income of the family. But Jesus insisted on traveling from place to place. Some support for this theory is found when Jesus appears to have briefly made Peter's home in Capernaum the center of his ministry. Peter awoke one morning and could not find Jesus. He located the Lord at some distance from Peter's home where he had spent much of the night in prayer. Peter told him, *"Everyone is looking for you!"* In other words, a crowd had gathered at Peter's home and wanted Jesus' attention. Jesus answered Peter saying, *"Let us go on to the neighboring towns, so that I may proclaim the message there also; for that is what I came out to do."* (Mark 1:38). Jesus "came out" from Peter's home rather than be settled in one place which is what his family may have wanted him to do.

It is possible that Jesus' family felt he was taking great risks following his ministry plan in which he was often critical of powerful people and institutions. Perhaps to save him from danger, they wanted to take him home where he would be safe. The family structure of that time was dominated by the father under strongly held traditions. Jesus saw this as detrimental to his call for total devotion to the personal rule of God. He makes this clear in the following: *"Anyone who loves his father or mother more than me is not worthy of me; anyone who loves his son or daughter more than me is not worthy of me."* (Matt 10:37-39). When Jesus uses the term *"more than me,"* in the above, he is not substituting himself in the place of God. Instead, he is asserting himself as the spokesperson for God.

In the Mediterranean world of that time, the family structure was not designed for the democratic development of children; it was structured for power, from the father on down. It is difficult for us to understand that sons and daughters were not free to accept Jesus' message and follow him without their father's permission. Jesus called for a new family structure, flowing out of the acceptance, encouragement and compassionate love of God, built on radical equality in which each individual had direct contact with others and with God. All are members together in the family of God.

Another surprising development is found in Jesus' practice of spending time with people who were diseased, maimed, outcasts and sinners. This practice included the poor, tax collectors and prostitutes, all of which angered some of the "good" people. And yet, sadly, in later years the church would often be divided according to class, sex, wealth and power.

In an age when men ruled, Jesus surprised many and undoubtedly angered some by reaching out to women and including them in his company. We are told in Luke's Gospel that a small group of wealthy women provided material support for his mission: *"Mary (called Magdalene), Joanna the wife of Cuza, the manager of Herod's household, Susanna and many others. These women were helping to support them out of their own means."* (Luke 8:2-3).When Jesus was crucified, devoted women were present: *"All his acquaintances and the women who had followed him from Galilee stood at a distance and saw these things."* (Luke 23:49)

Another surprise in the ministry of Jesus is the time it took. The first three Gospels tell us that it may have lasted only 15 months, while Buddha's work lasted 45 years, Muhammad established Islam in 20 years and Moses took 40 years to launch Israel as the covenant people of God. When Rome crucified Jesus, they might have thought it was the end of this peasant upstart from Galilee. But it appears to have taken less than 10 years for Christians to be living in Rome. In only 30 years, followers of Jesus were being persecuted in Rome by Emperor Nero, who blamed the terrible fire of Rome on the Christians, even though many of Rome's leaders placed the blame for starting the fire squarely on Nero himself, in order to clear land for the building of his golden home. While Nero is gone, the Christians he severely persecuted were the beginning of a movement of God, which is still going forward today. The God of Jesus is winning.

This Is My Beloved Son

10

Chapter 3

NOT A FAIRY TALE

"Once upon a time," a time which the Apostle Paul and others say was the right time, the Spirit of God moved silently to bless a newborn child. The Spirit no doubt moves to bless every baby, girl or boy. But this child, a boy child, though normal in every way, was destined for an amazing life, as later events would show. The tragedy and sorrow at the end of his life might have led some to conclude that it was not the Spirit of God which blessed this child, but an evil spirit from some black hole in the universe which had slipped in to curse and not bless. Others might look at the lives this child later blessed - the poor and the rich, the proud and the failures - and conclude that God was active in this life in a most remarkable way, as the following words from the Apostle Paul suggest: *"In Christ God was reconciling* [restoring, once again calling] *the world to himself."* (2 Cor 5:19).

But for the moment, this newborn child is aware of something new; he is hungry, and without thinking, he gropes with his mouth for his mother's breast. She is hardly old enough to have breasts, and yet it is with a feeling of delight that she offers what she has to her little boy. And it worked; the child grew.

But now it is time to close the curtain on his early life, for we only know with certainty that he grew up in the town of Nazareth, his parents were Joseph and Mary and he had four brothers whose names are given in Mt 13:55 as "James, Joseph, Simon, and Judas," and sisters who are not named.

His name was Jesus, son of a carpenter, who may have been a carpenter himself, for each Gospel gives us a slightly different reading:

Mark 6:3: *"Isn't this the carpenter? Isn't this Mary's son?"*
Matt 13:55: *"Isn't this the carpenter's son? His mother's name is Mary."*
Luke 4:22 RSV: *"Isn't this Joseph's son...?"*
John 1:45 RSV: *"Jesus of Nazareth, the son of Joseph."*

He knew about poverty since he and his family probably came from the large peasant class. Since Jesus and his father, Joseph, were carpenters, they were in the narrow space between peasants and the expendables. From the beginning, Jesus would have been regarded by those above him as a person of little worth. However, there is evidence that scholars were often referred to as carpenters. It is therefore possible that Jesus and his father Joseph were not carpenters but engaged in work which entitled them to be called "scholars." If true, this would explain how Jesus was so well educated and informed.

But if Jesus did come from the peasant class as is usually assumed, then he probably received a minimal education provided for boys. His amazing knowledge of Jewish scripture, nature and life, indicates he was self-taught and that he had learned much from regular attendance at the Jewish synagogue. His teaching shows not only that he had an appreciation of nature, but that he was also fully aware of the social, religious and political life of his people. About ninety-five percent of the Jewish population was illiterate.

While we know nothing reliable about his youth, we can surmise that when he was in his twenties and heard about the activities of John the Baptist, he decided to leave home and learn about John first hand. John's message was a severe and uncompromising announcement of judgment soon to come. Although there was no joy in it, people from Jerusalem and all of Judea came to hear John. He roared at them, *"You brood of vipers! Who warned you to flee from the coming wrath? Produce fruit in keeping with repentance. And do not think you can say to yourselves, 'We have Abraham as our father.' I tell you that out of these stones God can raise up children for Abraham. The ax is already at the root of the trees, and every tree that does not produce good fruit will be cut down and thrown into the fire."* *(Matthew 3:7-10)* Many did repent and were baptized by John.

We do not know how much time Jesus spent with John, whether he might have been one of John's disciples or simply an observer, learning and evaluating the Baptist's ministry. We do know that he was baptized by the Baptist in the river Jordan, a baptism which has caused many Christians concern since John's baptism was for people who were required to confess their sins and live a changed life. This has always been a challenge to those who believe that Jesus was free from sin and had nothing to confess. Nevertheless, it cannot be denied that he was baptized by the Baptist and that it was a baptism which followed repentance for sin.

The Gospel of John is very different from the first three and while it includes the beliefs of Christians of a later time, most main-line scholars see it as far less reliable, historically, than the first three. John gives the impression that Jesus is baptized by the Baptist, but his baptism is not actually mentioned in John. There is considerable judgment in John's Gospel of those who do not believe that Jesus is the Son of God, *"Whoever believes in him is not condemned, but whoever does not believe stands condemned already because he has not believed in the name of God's one and only Son. This is the verdict: Light has come into the world, but men loved darkness instead of light because their deeds were evil."* (John 3:18-19). See also John 3:36 and John 5:28, 29 and other verses in the fourth Gospel.

Something amazing happened when Jesus was baptized. The three Gospels, Matthew, Mark and Luke, include the incident, but do not agree on exactly what happened. All three Gospels say that when Jesus was baptized, "a voice from heaven" spoke. In Matthew the voice said *"This is my son, the Beloved; with whom I am well pleased."* (Matthew 3:17 NRSV)

Note that Matthew tells us the voice declared to everyone present that Jesus was the beloved son of God. But Mark 1:11 and Luke 3:22 say the voice spoke only to Jesus and not to the crowd:

13

"You are my son, the beloved; with you I am well pleased." So which was it? Was the voice from heaven something which only Jesus experienced, or was it meant for everyone to hear? In John's Gospel, there is no voice; instead, John the Baptist sees the Spirit of God descend and remain on Jesus: *"The one who sent me to baptize with water told me, 'The man on whom you see the Spirit come down and remain is he who will baptize with the Holy Spirit.' I have seen and I testify that this is the Son of God."* (John 1:33-34)

It appears certain the voice spoke only to Jesus, for this was a great moment when he became convinced of a call from God to spend his life on an important mission, following the leading and inspiration of the Spirit of God. After the time spent with John the Baptist, *"Jesus returned to Galilee in the power of the Spirit."* (Luke 4:14)

We are informed by the Gospels through frequent references to the Spirit, that Jesus was a Spirit-led person, one who was intimately in touch with God the Holy Spirit. The Gospels record that he prayed often and while those times of prayer are not described in detail, we must assume they included times of silence, times of rehearsing the Spirit-inspired message and strategy for the days ahead, which came to him through a conscious opening of his mind to the holy God. The Gospels help us to understand that he did not act independently, for we are often told that he was led by the Spirit, especially in critical moments and at times of important decisions.

To be convinced that God was in Jesus' life in a unique way requires faith which is based on strong evidence, enabling us to move on in a careful examination of this amazing person's life. And for that we go back to the Jordan River, where John baptized the multitudes.

After Jesus was baptized, he went into the wilderness where he was tempted by Satan. The account of this event in the first three Gospels raises questions. Mark tells us that the spirit drove him into the wilderness while Matthew and Luke say he was not driven but "led" into the wilderness by the Spirit. Matthew goes on to say that Jesus ate nothing at all for 40 days, which might be enough to end in death. When it was over, Matthew and Luke, (but not Mark), inform us that *"angels ...waited on him,"* which conflicts with his humanity and cannot be regarded as historical. This will not bother us if we are willing to accept what dedicated Christian scholars tell us about how the four Gospels developed into their final form. More on this important subject later.

When we consider the wilderness temptations, we must first ask how the Gospel writers came into possession of this story, since Jesus was alone, with no one present to remember and pass on what happened. Unless we are willing to set the story aside as a Christian invention, we must conclude that Jesus himself told the story to his disciples at a later time. The story of the temptation is presented to us in symbolic language, much like the parables Jesus frequently used in his teaching.

In the synoptic Gospels, (Matthew, Mark and Luke), Mark says only that Jesus was tempted by Satan, and nothing more. Matthew and Luke contain all three of the temptations but not in the same order. We will follow Luke's order, where we are told that after not eating for 40 days, Jesus was famished. In Luke, the Devil said to him: *"If you are the son of God, command this stone to become a loaf of bread."* (Luke 4:3 NRSV). Even if we assume that Jesus had the power to turn stones into bread, it is difficult to believe he would do that simply to satisfy his hunger, which certainly could have been satisfied in other ways. He answered Satan by saying, *"It is written: 'Man does not live on bread alone."* (Luke 4:4 NRSV)

While there are many interpretations of what the temptations mean, they must surely have had a direct bearing on Jesus' belief that God had called him to an important mission to his people, which the "voice from Heaven" spoke to him when he was baptized. What follows has some merit.

Since his mission was first to his own people, he would have reflected on the painful fact that among his people, starvation was happening all the time for many living in destitution, in utter poverty. For thousands, starvation was only a bad harvest away. It is reasonable to believe that Jesus may have been thinking about how he could spend his energies and gifts in trying to end hunger and poverty among his people. But if so, he rejected that important cause knowing that the human condition runs deeper than hunger for food. As he continued to meditate and pray, he was led to conclude that the basic human hunger is for God and that this was the mission he was called to pursue. Jesus recalled a saying from the Jewish Bible in Deuteronomy, *"Man does not live on bread alone but on every word that comes from the mouth of the LORD."* (Deut 8:3). He rejected the temptation to spend his energies and gifts in overcoming the scourge of human hunger and starvation. No stones were turned into bread.

In the second temptation, the Devil took Jesus up on a high mountain and *"showed him all the kingdoms of the world in a moment of time. Then Satan said to him, 'I will give you all their authority and splendor, for it has been given to me, and I can give it to anyone I want to. So if you worship me, it will all be yours.'"* (Luke 4:6-7). Once again Jesus responds with a passage from Deuteronomy 6:13, *"You shall worship the Lord your God, and him only you shall serve."* (Matthew 4:10).

This temptation cannot be taken literally for there was no way Jesus could be tempted to worship Satan. A possible explanation is that Jesus knew people are human and burdened with many pressures, so why not compromise his message by making it easy to accept. It is possible that he may also have been tempted to recognize the cruel power of the Roman Empire and the sufferings of his people and the readiness of many of them to revolt if only the right leader could be found. But however it might be justified, to Jesus this would be a denial of his intimate relationship with the Father, a relationship so valuable to him it could never be compromised. It was also contrary to what he wanted for his burdened people. Later he would make it abundantly clear that his mission did not include violence. He rejected the temptation to compromise his message and mission. Later he would tell his disciples that to follow him meant they would have to make many sacrifices and even be ready to bear a cross. *"Anyone who does not carry his cross and follow me cannot be my disciple."* (Luke 14:27).

In the third temptation the Devil took Jesus to the highest point of the Temple and said to him, *"If you are the Son of God, throw yourself down from here. For it is written: 'He will command his angels concerning you to guard you carefully; they will lift you up in their hands, so that you will not strike your foot against a stone.'"* (Luke 4:9-11). Note that the Devil is now quoting Scripture. Jesus ended the temptations by saying, *"You shall not tempt the Lord your God."* Don't you think it is impossible to believe that Jesus could actually have been tempted to jump off the roof of the Temple, just to see if angels would come to rescue him before he hit the ground? Again, we need to remember in his baptism Jesus had received confirmation of a call from God to pursue a great mission for his people and that he lived in a violent time and place. It would not be long before his friend, John the baptizer, would be arrested and later executed. Jesus must have recognized the personal risks involved in answering God's call. He could have been tempted to expect God's protection if he threw himself wholeheartedly not off the top of the Temple but into the task to which he was summoned. His decision was to obey God's call, accept the risks involved and put his whole trust in the "abba" father. He understood that the men and women who would later answer his call, would also be required to put their trust in God despite the risks, so how could he do anything less? He rejected the third temptation to expect God's protection as he pursued his mission. Luke says the devil *"departed from him until an opportune time."*

Once again, John's gospel does not show Jesus being tempted. That is what we have come to expect from John, for he never presents Jesus in any compromising situation, such as submitting to a baptism for the forgiveness of sins, or being tempted by anything or anyone. Notice that in John's Gospel, Jesus is completely in charge of everything that happens.

This Is My Beloved Son

Chapter 4

BEGINNING IN GALILEE

According to the synoptic Gospels, the ministry of Jesus began when the work of John the Baptist came to an end, although the Gospel of John has Jesus carrying on a ministry with his disciples in Judea including the baptism of converts. This was in the same general area where John baptized people: *"After this, Jesus and his disciples went out into the Judean countryside, where he spent some time with them, and baptized."* (John 3:22) Also from John, *"They (*John's disciples*) came to John and said to him, 'Rabbi, that man who was with you on the other side of the Jordan – the one you testified about – well, he is baptizing, and everyone is going to him.'"* (John 3:26). In the material which follows, we will be using the information from the synoptic Gospels: Matthew, Mark and Luke. They tell us that when John the Baptizer was arrested and imprisoned by King Herod, Jesus left the desert near the Jordan River and returned to Galilee.

Apparently when Jesus meditated on his calling, he concluded that God had led him to a different message from that of the Baptist. John's message was one of judgment, warning people to avoid the coming wrath of God. To Jesus, God was accepting, encouraging, under-standing and full of grace and love. This message, centering in the God of compassion, was the good news he carried with him to Galilee.

Not only was Jesus' message different from John's, his style of living was radically different. John was an ascetic who ate sparingly and lived in the Jordan River wilderness, while Jesus embraced the goodness of life by enjoying both food and drink and the company of others, including the presence of those whom the

19

religious elite spurned. His critics not only denounced him for spending time with such people, but they were especially critical because he even ate with them. To associate with and especially eat with people who were regarded as outcasts and sinners was to do a shameful thing in a society which put great emphasis on avoiding shameful behavior. Jesus was convinced God loved and accepted these people, so how could he do any less?

Some scholars are convinced that Jesus must have led a rather impoverished life, even though he enjoyed the good life when possible. He had no money, even though there was a group of wealthy women who supplied some of his needs. There were no motels, so where did he sleep? Since he and his disciples were occasionally invited into the home of an admirer, we can only surmise he might have had some shelter in cold weather. We do not know how often there was food, although there is evidence that people in the crowds were often willing to share what they had. When someone indicated a willingness to follow Jesus, he replied, *"Foxes have holes, and birds of the air have nests; but the Son of Man has nowhere to lay his head."* (Luke 9:58 RSV). Some scholars say that in a different context, Jesus' statement could mean that only humans – (Son of Man is a term indicating a human) – can be homeless, since foxes and birds have a den or a nest to call home. Meanwhile, where did Jesus and the disciples go when it rained? We can only conclude that Jesus and his disciples spent many nights sleeping on the ground. Fortunately, the climate was normally mild.

While the Gospels of Matthew, Mark and Luke do not agree on the details concerning Jesus' ministry in Galilee, collectively they tell us much more about Jesus' thinking and what moved and motivated him than we find in the records of all of the important personalities of ancient times. We know that Jesus spoke like one of the prophets of ancient Israel, reminding people of their responsibilities to God and one another. He also had a reputation as a popular healer and exorcist. People came to him with their illnesses and somehow he was able to help them. His reputation spread quickly and we are told crowds gathered everywhere he went. Apparently more came for healing or to witness a healing than to hear Jesus' message. But they did hear it and a few were ready to hear more. He did not remain in one location, but moved from place to place in an effort to spread his message far and wide. John the Baptist had people come to him, but Jesus took his good news to the people.

Near the beginning of his work in Galilee, he called twelve men to be with him to be his disciples and to expand his mission. Jesus' followers were not limited to the twelve, for there were many men and women, some of whom were wealthy and educated, who joined the larger group of admirers, though they apparently did not travel with him. We are also told he trained 70 others whom he sent out to adjoining villages in Galilee to expand his mission. While the disciples were often presented by the Gospel writers as slow learners, they became the foundation stones of the infant Christian church which came into existence following his resurrection. We owe our faith and knowledge of Jesus to them.

The best way to understanding the mission and message of Jesus is in his amazing relationship with God. It was more than believing God exists; he experienced God in an intimate and personal way. What he practiced and taught was in imitation of the God he knew in his times of prayer and meditation. God was the central reality, as real as the disciples and his critics. His unique experience of God was the foundation of his absolute certainty of God. Everything he said and did can be traced back to this experience. Christianity is a religion based, not on correct beliefs or theology, but on experience. There are millions of Christians today who can testify to their own experience of God. Most of them will say they experience God best through their experience of Jesus, who gives the clearest introduction we have to the God of goodness and love. Jesus is not confined to the New Testament. He is alive and with us, still leading his present-day disciples, just as he was experienced by those first Christians in the days and years after the resurrection.

Jesus nearly always referred to himself as the "Son of Man." One time he asked the disciples what people were saying about him and Peter answered for the others. In Matthew's Gospel, Peter said *"You are the Christ, the Son of the Living God."* In Mark, Peter said, *"You are the Messiah,"* while Luke records, *"You are the Messiah of God."* Matthew frequently inserts material which reflects the beliefs of Christians in the church which existed at the time his Gospel was written, but which was not always true at the time Jesus lived and taught in Galilee. That is why Matthew had Peter add that Jesus not only is the Christ, but also *"the Son of the Living God."* Mark and Luke do the same only not as often as Matthew. The term "Son of God" occurs over one hundred times in the Gospel of John which declares Jesus to be the Messiah in the first chapter and repeatedly throughout the Gospel. In the synoptic Gospels, Jesus never says *"I am the Messiah,"* and he says he is the Son of God only once, when he is examined by the High Priest, who quickly condemned him, accusing him of blasphemy, deserving of death, a charge which was not true. In the Hebrew Scriptures, the King was often referred to as God's son.

When Jesus called himself the "Son of Man" he was simply saying he was human or a human being, thereby identifying with his audience. We see "Son of Man" used in Psalm 8:4. The NIV translates the Psalm: *"What is man that you are mindful of him, the son of man that you care for him?"* The New Revised Standard Bible says, *"What are human beings that you are mindful of them, mortals that you care for them?"* The NIV gives the literal translation while the NRSV provides the accurate meaning. Psalm 8 extols the wonder of human beings in sharp contrast to the Genesis account of the creation of the first humans who immediately sin and are cursed. Psalm 8 adds this surprising thought, addressed to God, *"You have made them, (*humans*), a little lower than God, and crowned them with glory and honor."* (Psalm 8:4-5 NRSV). Psalm 8 is more in keeping with Jesus' estimate of human worth, as we shall see.

Jesus often acted or spoke against the domination system, though he never used that term. Throughout the Roman Empire about 2 % of the people owned most of the land with the rest of the population organized so that wealth flowed upward to those at the top. The owners of large tracts of land provided the leaders who ran the government. Religious Priests owned about 12 – 15 % of the land. Both land owning groups were supported by those in the lower classes. Military generals, bureaucrats and merchants did not own land and were important but submissive to those above them, while they in turn dominated those under them. Each population strata had others above them who dominated them, and population layers under them whom they dominated. At the bottom were the peasants who were the vast majority of the population and who were forced to contribute two-thirds of their annual crop to support those above them. Under the peasants were the artisans who often came from the peasants who had lost their land and had become day laborers, doing whatever they could to make a living. At the very bottom were the expendable people - beggars, outlaws, day laborers and slaves. An undetermined number of these folk simply perished each year. Jesus' experience of God set him in opposition to this whole domination system.

Jesus knew the wealthy were among those who exercised harmful control over the poor, exacting as much as they could from them to maintain their wealth. He made it abundantly clear that the wealthy would have an almost impossible entrance into the kingdom of God.

As already mentioned, his message of the God of grace and compassion was a major departure from the accepted understanding of God's ways. We can be sure that it was from his own experience in prayer and meditation that Jesus discovered the kindness, compassion and encouragement of the Heavenly Father. It can be summarized in the statement that "God loves sinners." Some of the Priests and Pharisees would agree that God loves the sinners who repent, keep the Sabbath and make the right sacrifices in the Temple and eating the right food. But Jesus taught that God loves sinners even before they repent. God's love and acceptance comes first. This understanding was radical then and is still radical for many today, but it can be clearly demonstrated from Jesus' own teaching.

In Mark's Gospel, Jesus said, *"Whoever wants to save his life will lose it, but whoever loses his life for me and for the gospel will save it."* (Mark 8:35). Jesus was not referring to losing one's life as the result of violent persecution, or by becoming a martyr in a valiant attempt to overthrow the Romans. Instead, he was emphasizing the need to take one's self out of the center of life by putting God at the center. The word "gospel" means "good news" and the good news is that God is fully trustworthy and compassionate and can be trusted for life and death. Although we have no record that Jesus ever said it, the core of his message was, "He who loses his life in God, will find life."

While Jesus' efforts appeared to be successful at first, it soon became obvious that his ministry was in peril from people of power. When Jesus spoke constantly about the kingdom of God, King Herod would surely have taken notice and undoubtedly would have felt that talk about another kingdom was a threat to his rule. Some friendly Pharisees warned Jesus one time that Herod had indicated he wished to see Jesus, meaning Herod wanted to have him arrested and killed. Jesus traveled beyond Galilee, when this warning came, to avoid Herod's grasp. When he returned, he continued his ministry and then began the long journey to Jerusalem where the danger was even greater.

It was very difficult for some in the crowds to understand and adopt his gospel. Many probably felt that Jesus' message was too radical for them and they lacked the inner resolve to make the changes in thinking which he called for. For centuries his people had experienced God as caring and forgiving, but also as vindictive and threatening. They often interpreted the calamities in their history and the tragedies in their personal lives as the direct action of God. This led some to conclude that sickness and poverty was proof of God's punishment. As a consequence of this belief, those who were trying to live the faith as fully as possible not only rejoiced in their righteousness, but made it clear that those who were not trying as hard or not trying at all were simply lost. They called them sinners and outcasts which meant some could not even be thought of as Jews anymore but as Gentiles. In Galilee, Jesus' opponents were the Scribes and Pharisees, though he had some friends among them. Large crowds followed him wherever he went, people who were attracted to his exorcisms and healings, but also to his good news.

What was there in Jesus' message which brought forth both curiosity and condemnation? We deal with this question in depth in later chapters on the teaching of Jesus and the kingdom of God. But first we consider the long and often sad record of the Jewish people.

This Is My Beloved Son

Chapter 5

THE HISTORY OF JESUS' PEOPLE

Jewish history begins with the patriarch Abraham, who was regarded as the father of the Hebrew people. His story is found in the book of Genesis, beginning in chapter 12. God made a covenant, a binding agreement with Abraham, which was renewed with his son Isaac and with Isaac's son Jacob, whose name was changed to Israel. Jacob's twelve sons were called the children of Israel, as were all his many descendants. Israel (Jacob) moved to Egypt when his son Joseph was the Prime Minister under the Pharaoh. In time, the children of Israel were reduced to slavery. Under the leadership of Moses, the Israelites were led out of Egypt to freedom, an event which they never forgot. Through Moses, they were given God's laws, including the Ten Commandments as part of a new covenant between God and the people.

When Moses died, Joshua led the Israelites in the conquest of "the Promised Land." While the book of Joshua tells us the conquest was quickly completed, we know it took a few generations, some covered in the book of Judges. They were struggling to stay united and defend themselves against strong enemies. Samuel was the last of the Judges, who reluctantly yielded to the demands of the people and anointed Saul as their first King. With some help from Samuel, King Saul was able to mold the tribes together into a nation. When Saul was killed in battle, David became King and succeeded not only in uniting the ten northern tribes with his own tribes of Judah and Benjamin, but through numerous conquests of neighboring people, he produced a strong nation, with Jerusalem as the capital.

David was succeeded by his son Solomon who reigned over a

nation at peace, with great prosperity. After Solomon, the ten northern tribes split away from Judah and Benjamin and formed their own nation with its capital in Samaria. A long period of time followed, sometimes with peace and cooperation between the two Israelite countries, but other times of unrest and warfare. Meanwhile, the time had passed when small countries could go about their business in relative peace. Mighty empires were rising, each one determined to expand its borders through conquest, no matter how many weaker peoples were cruelly slaughtered. And there was always the ancient Egyptian kingdom in the South along the Nile, which exerted a strong influence in the Middle East.

The Assyrians, north of Judah and Israel, rose in power, with their capital at Nineveh. The Assyrians conquered the kingdom of Israel in 721 BCE, marching off hundreds of its citizens, marking the end of Israel as a nation. These ten tribes are occasionally referred to as the lost tribes of Israel, since they were never reconstituted as a separate people.

The tiny kingdom of Judah, with its capital in Jerusalem, continued on for some time, though constantly threatened by the Egyptians in the South and rising empires in the North. The Assyrians were overcome by the Babylonian empire, with its capital in the city of Babylon. Under the Babylonian King Nebuchadnezzar, Jerusalem was destroyed, the Temple burned and hundreds of the people killed or sent into exile in the capital city of Babylon in the years around 586 BCE. Zedekiah was made King of Judah by Nebuchadnezzar at the age of 21. After nine years, Zedekiah rebelled, but was soon subdued by the Babylonian King. At the age of 31, Zedekiah's young sons were killed in his presence and then he was blinded by Nebuchadnezzar.

Few things last forever. Babylon was quickly and surprisingly overcome by the Medes and Persians under the leadership of Cyrus the Great, who decreed that captive peoples could return to their homeland if they desired. Many, but not all the captives from Judah, (now called Jews), returned to Jerusalem and began the slow and difficult task of rebuilding the walls of the city and then a Temple.

Years later, Alexander the Great defeated Persia and took possession of the Middle East. The Jewish people found themselves under a new master.

After the death of Alexander, his vast conquered lands were divided among his generals. The Jews in Palestine came under the rule of Ptolemy I of Egypt. Later, the Selucid family took control of Palestine. They attempted to force the Jews to adopt Greek ways. When a pig was sacrificed in the Jerusalem Temple, a Jewish priest named Mattathias, together with his sons, revolted successfully and the Jews were able to regain their independence. But it was taken away again when the Romans, under Pompey, extended Roman rule over the whole area in 63BCE. They were still there in the time of Jesus.

It was during the captivity in Babylon that the Synagogue began since Solomon's Temple had been destroyed. While worship took place in the Synagogue, sacrifices were not offered. The Synagogue was used as a general purpose building where people gathered to share news, listen to lectures, debate with one another and also worship God. Boys went to school in the Synagogue. It had many of the uses of a town hall. There was a head of the Synagogue who was sometimes a priest who may have led worship and delivered messages. Lay people could perform all these functions provided they were equipped with learning, especially the Jewish Bible (Old Testament). A visitor could be asked if he had something to say. Jesus was often invited to speak in synagogues.

There are long periods of time in the above outline of Jewish history during which we have little or no information. In Protestant Bibles, we have nothing during the 400 years after the Jewish people returned to Jerusalem from captivity in Babylon. Outside the Old Testament, there are writings of varying degrees of helpfulness, though scholars regularly study them.

Jesus' people looked back over their history and saw with great pride that Yahweh had chosen them to be his own people. They recalled how God said through Moses: *"Thus you shall say to the house of Jacob, and tell the people of Israel: You have seen what I did to the Egyptians, and how I bore you on eagles' wings and brought you to myself. Now therefore, if you will obey my voice and keep my covenant, you shall be my own possession among all peoples; for all the earth is mine and you shall be to me a kingdom of priests and a holy nation."* (Ex 19:3-6 RSV).

In its simplest form, the Covenant was an agreement or contract between God and the Children of Israel. For their part, the people promised to worship Yahweh alone, and to keep his commandments. Yahweh was God's name, often written as YHWH. In return, God promised to be their God, to protect and prosper them as long as they were faithful to the covenant. But Yahweh also promised to punish and curse the people if they failed to be faithful. The best known summary of the Law is the Ten Commandments found in Exodus 20:1-17, and Deuteronomy 5:6-21. In addition, there are three somewhat different legal codes: the Covenant Code in Exodus 20:22- 23:33, the Deuteronomic Code in Deuteronomy chapters 12-26 and the Holiness Code in Leviticus Chapters 17-26.

While all people in ancient times believed in supernatural beings and many gods, the Jews were monotheists who believed in only one God. Although he was especially their God who had chosen them as his own people, they initially believed his rule was limited to their own lands. Later they came to believe his rule extended over the whole world.

All peoples in ancient times had temples or sacred places for worship. It was under Moses that the Tabernacle was built as the exiles wandered through the wilderness for forty years. The Tabernacle was for the sacrifice of animals offered by the people for the forgiveness of sins. Years later, in the reign of King Solomon, a temple was built in Jerusalem in place of the Tabernacle. All males were required to attend temple worship at least three times each year, though in the time of Jesus, with Jews scattered throughout the Roman world, this requirement could no longer be enforced.

The Jewish Temple was distinctive since there was no image of God in it. Gentiles thought the absence of an idol was extremely odd, not only because there was no image of the Jewish God, YHWH, but Jews did not include the gods of the Greeks and Romans as most other people did in their Temples. The Ark of the Covenant was their most sacred object which was lost when the nation suffered defeat. The Ark was a box about six feet long, with poles on each side for carrying, made of special wood, covered with gold. On either end of the Ark was a cherub, an angelic figure, also covered with gold, each kneeling, facing each other, with wings unfurled above them, with their wing tips touching. This was to help people understand why they could not have a visual image of God, for God was in the empty space between the angels. Unlike the gods of other peoples, YHWH could not be revealed to the eyes through any representation of wood, clay or stone.

To enter the Temple, worshippers had to purify themselves from contact with a corpse, childbirth or bodily emissions. In the time of Jesus, washing one's hands before or after eating was adopted by some, the goal of which was not cleanliness, but ritual cleanness. Jesus' disciples were accused of not washing their hands before eating, to which Jesus quoted Isaiah 29:13, *"These people honor me with their lips, but their hearts are far from me."* (Mark 7:6).

To the Jewish people, everything in life was covered by their religious beliefs. But since the Law of Moses was unclear on specifics, interpretation of its meaning was required. In Jesus' day the interpreters of the Law were the Priests and the Pharisees who relied on their Scribes for understanding. The Priests were the only people who could offer the sacrifices in the Temple, aided by the Levites, a separate class of Jews whose purpose was to assist the Priests. Both Priests and Levites took turns when on duty and were only partially supported by the temple tax and tithes, requiring them to have other jobs for their support, except farming.

Jesus' people wanted to love God with all their heart, mind and strength while also living under the shadow of God's awful wrath. Fear of God was one cornerstone of their religious practice as these verses indicate: *"Know and see that it is evil and bitter for you to forsake the LORD your God; the fear of me is not in you, says the Lord GOD of hosts,"* (Jeremiah 2:19 RSV). Also, *"Moses said to the people, 'Do not be afraid. God has come to test you, so that the fear of God will be with you to keep you from sinning.'"* (Ex 20:20). Faithful Jews repeated the Shema twice every day: *"Hear, O Israel: The LORD our God is one LORD; and you shall love the LORD your God with all your heart, and with all your soul, and with all your might."* (Deut 6:4-5 RSV).

But almost from the beginning the Israelites failed to keep the covenant with YHWH their God. In fact, there is strong evidence to show that the chosen people, as they liked to think of themselves, never fully grasped the ultimate extent of the covenant. When God made the covenant with Abraham he said: *"I will make you into a great nation and I will bless you; I will make your name great, and you will be a blessing. I will bless those who bless you, and whoever curses you I will curse; and all peoples on earth will be blessed through you."* (Gen 12:2-3).

The ultimate goal was the blessing of all the earth's peoples through the descendants of Abraham. But when we consider the violence of ancient times and the appearance of cities and the rule of powerful men who mobilized their people to forcibly take what their neighbors had, we can readily see how difficult it was for anyone to embrace the ultimate terms of the call to Abraham. Still, this lofty goal appears to have been present very early among them. The goal was the blessing of all peoples through the descendants of Abraham.

The Covenant with Abraham set a high standard, but later in Deuteronomy the people are given a short lesson in humility, but nothing is said about being a blessing to the world: *"The LORD did not set his affection on you and choose you because you were more numerous than other peoples, for you were the fewest of all peoples. But it was because the LORD loved you and kept the oath he swore to your forefathers that he brought you out with a mighty hand and redeemed you from the land of slavery, from the power of Pharaoh king of Egypt"* (Deut 7:7-8). God's promise to Abraham that all families of the earth would be blessed through his descendants is not recalled.

Psalm 46 speaks of a longing for peace, *"Come and see the works of the LORD, the desolations he has brought on the earth. He makes wars cease to the ends of the earth; he breaks the bow and shatters the spear, he burns the shields with fire."* (Psalm 46:8-9). But the very next Psalm has a very different focus: *"How awesome is the LORD Most High, the great King over all the earth! He subdued nations under us, peoples under our feet."* (Psalm 47:2-3). How quickly the emphasis changes from God who "makes wars cease" to God "who subdues nations under us."

Psalms 67 says the reason God has blessed his people is so that God's *"ways may be known on earth, your salvation among all nations."* (Psalm 67:2). The prophet Isaiah looked forward to a time when God *"will judge between the nations and will settle disputes for many peoples. They will beat their swords into plowshares and their spears into pruning hooks."* (Isaiah 2:4). He also says that in this peaceful time to come, *"nation will not take up sword against nation, nor will they train for war anymore."* That time is yet to come.

But the failure to share with other nations and peoples the ways of the Covenant God, was nullified when the Israelite people often failed to practice love and justice even with one another. The prophets frequently denounced the people for the lack of justice in their treatment of the weaker members of society. In the first chapter of Isaiah's prophecy, he said: *"Take your evil deeds out of my sight! Stop doing wrong, learn to do right! Seek justice, encourage the oppressed. Defend the cause of the fatherless, plead the case of the widow."* (Isaiah 1:16-17). The prophet Amos also spoke against injustice: *"Take away from me the noise of your songs; I will not listen to the melody of your harps. But let justice roll down like waters, and righteousness like an ever-flowing stream."* (Amos 5:23-24). Micah issued the same call: *"He has showed you, O man, what is good. And what does the LORD require of you? To act justly and to love mercy and to walk humbly with your God."* (Micah 6:8)

The Prophets had warned the people in their day that God's

wrath would fall upon them because they had forgotten their covenant with God and because the wealthy and powerful had failed to treat the poor with justice. The Prophet Jeremiah spoke of God's coming punishment: *"Therefore this is what the LORD says: 'I will bring on them a disaster they cannot escape. Although they cry out to me, I will not listen to them.'"* (Jer. 11:11).

Jesus' good news represented too much of a departure from what many regarded as the essentials of the faith. In a surprisingly short time the mood of the accounts in the synoptic Gospels changed to one of growing danger. Near the end of his time in Galilee, Jesus began the journey to Jerusalem with his disciples and other followers. Soon after his arrival he was condemned and crucified. Why was Jesus crucified? Before we can consider the answer to that vexing question, we will consider the social and political environment which prevailed in the time of Jesus and the religious convictions and practices of his people.

Chapter 6

THE SOCIAL AND POLITICAL CLIMATE

In Jesus' day his people still carried with them the conviction that they were special in God's eyes, but they also lived under the burden of guilt for having disobeyed God many times, which, they believed, was why they were not free. But when we consider the turbulent times which existed for much of their history, we wonder how the children of Israel could possibly think of sharing with others faith in God and the Covenant, while often faced with enemies who wanted to destroy them.

Much of their religious life in Jesus' day was set up on the basis of rewards and punishments. Some believed in life after death, but most believed rewards or punishments were experienced in this life only. When people did well and prospered, that meant God had blessed them as a reward for their faithful living. But if a person was poor or sick, many believed it was because he or she had failed God in some way and their condition was God's punishment. Jesus acted to free people from this belief.

One's identity was established largely by boundaries: Jews versus Gentiles, Jews versus Samaritans, and sinners versus the righteous. This produced a hierarchical order in society, which was very rigid: men over women, oldest son over younger sons, wealthy over the poor, land owners over the landless, powerful over the weak. The successful were righteous; those who failed were the wicked.

In Palestine, two worlds were in conflict; one was Jewish culture and Jewish political life, and the other was Greek culture and Roman political power. Among the wealthier Jews, especially the Sadducees, the Greek culture was often adopted, much to the distress of those Jews who were trying to maintain the ancient customs and ways of their people. The Roman Government was very oppressive, ruling often with terror tactics, heavy taxes and the daily humiliations which are part of an occupying power. To make matters worse, the governors assigned to Palestine were of inferior rank, often incompetent, corrupt, and antagonistic toward Jewish ways. One of the worst was Governor Pilate who ruled 26-36 CE, during the time of Jesus, and who ordered Jesus' scourging and crucifixion. Jesus was crucified by the Romans and emphatically not by the Jews, who did not have the legal authority to execute.

There was double taxation since taxes were required by the religious establishment and by the Romans. The religious tax of over 20% annually was used to support the Jerusalem priests and Temple worship, in addition to the Roman occupation tax plus customs, tolls and tributes. Jewish and Roman taxes together equaled about 35%. Rome collected taxes through Jewish tax collectors from whom they demanded a fixed amount; anything over that was the tax collector's income. Roman power made sure that taxes were collected. There was no penalty if the Jewish tithe and taxes were not paid and many simply could not pay. If Roman taxes were not paid, a farmer's land could be taken, which created landless day laborers, robbers and beggars. The same loss of land could befall people who were forced by circumstances to borrow from wealthier Jewish citizens. When the debt grew to the place it could not be repaid, land and home were often forfeited or the debtor became a day laborer. Jews who refused or who could not pay the Temple taxes were regarded as non-observant Jews and called sinners and treated as outcasts and Gentiles.

Since God is holy, God's people were to be holy too. Holy means "separate from." Yahweh's demand that the people be holy was interpreted to mean separation from everything considered to defile or make impure. Food and clothing and even people were divided into clean or unclean, pure or impure, sacred or profane, Jew or Gentile, righteous or sinner. Many Jews believed that a lack of holiness and purity is why they were often defeated and were subject peoples. As a result, many almost desperately wanted to live right to avoid God's wrath and not be swallowed up by another culture. They tried hard to keep separate from other peoples, which brought considerable persecution upon them in parts of the empire where they were a minority.

There were four groups among Palestinian Jews: Sadducees, Essenes, Pharisees and Zealots. The Sadducees were conservative, wealthy, aristocratic and not supportive of any renewal efforts. They were the wealthiest group in Jewish society, who tended to adopt some of the Greek culture and therefore were not anxious to see things changed.

Next were the Essenes, who believed in total separation, even from other Jews. They were a renewal group, but were so devoted to holiness that they did not even associate with their own people. They are best known through the discovery of the Dead Sea Scrolls at a desert place called Qumran on the western shore of the Dead Sea. Because they were convinced that a life of holiness was not possible within society, many withdrew to the wilderness. The Essenes looked for the coming of two Messiahs, one like King David and the other like Aaron, the first High Priest, who was the brother of Moses. In the Essene view, the Kingly Messiah did nothing while the Priestly Messiah was in charge.

The next group was the Pharisees who truly tried to be holy, and to help their people be true to the faith. The laws with regard to tithing and purity tended to be their main focus. They would not even eat untithed food, that is, 1/10th of the food must have been dedicated to God. They had no legal power to force others to pay the tithe, which they still tried to enforce through social and religious ostracism. The ultimate punishment for the non-observant person was to be regarded as a Gentile or an outcast. They would not eat with them or allow them to sit on local councils and no longer regarded them as "Children of Abraham." But the Pharisees produced some of the best in Judaism. They gave absolute loyalty to God as they understood God, including love of neighbor, Sabbath joy, Jewish festivals, prayer and fasting. Those they called outcasts were the worst of the sinners: murderers, prostitutes including those who refused or were unable to tithe or observe religious obligations. Some of the more righteous Pharisees were not sure if the outcasts could ever be saved, even though they were not sure if there was any life beyond this life.

The fourth group, according to the Jewish historian Josephus, was the resistance fighters, called Zealots, who often erupted in violence, usually led by a charismatic leader who believed God would not act to restore their nation until they demonstrated their faithfulness by taking violent action to expel the Romans, which some called "Forcing the End." The leaders were often people who had already lost everything and so had little to lose except life itself. Every time they tried, their efforts resulted in defeat, with many killed or crucified. Led by the Zealots, the Jewish people rebelled against Rome twice, in 66-73 CE and in 123 - 135 CE. Both times they were eventually crushed by the Roman military power and thousands were killed. We know Jesus had supporters among the Pharisees and Zealots, but none are known among the Sadducees or Essenes.

Most people in the Roman Empire lived in an honor and shame society, in which individuals tended to evaluate themselves as they imagined others saw them. The opinions of others determined one's own existence. If the individual felt he had somehow lost the honor of others, he automatically lost all honor for himself. A person with leprosy was so completely devoid of respect and honor that he was regarded as already dead, but still walking. Jesus did not depend on others for his honorable opinion of himself; he received his honor from his certainty of God's love and acceptance, which he longed for others to discover and enjoy. But how could an individual say yes to Jesus if his family or friends said no. He would run the risk of losing his selfhood, his standing in the family and community, which explains why more people did not embrace Jesus and his message.

Going all the way back to Abraham, Jews circumcised their infant sons. In the time of Jesus, some Greek customs were adopted by wealthier Jews, including the gymnasium which required male nakedness. As a result, some Jewish men tried to eliminate the marks of circumcision.

The interpreters of the Law occasionally found interesting ways to work around the Law's literal intent. The prophet Jeremiah had forbidden carrying food from their homes on the Sabbath. But families liked to get together to share a meal on the Sabbath, the only day free from work. To meet the letter of Jeremiah's Law, they built a series of doors & lintels between the houses, which meant that when food was taken from one house to another, it never actually left the "house," since they were all connected as one.

They had a neat way of coping with a tooth ache. They were forbidden from putting vinegar on it if the ache developed on the Sabbath. So they put vinegar on their food and got the same beneficial result. Fighting enemies on the Sabbath presented another challenge. When they refused to fight on the Sabbath, the result was defeat. They finally decided that when faced with attack, they could defend themselves without breaking the Sabbath Law.

While the Romans exercised ultimate control, the High Priest was responsible for peace and order in Jerusalem. This was especially needed during important worship occasions when Jerusalem was crowded with people. The High Priest knew that if any riot or disruption occurred, the Roman soldiers would be unleashed and Jewish lives would be lost. It was a heavy responsibility for the High Priest. For all Rome's vaunted glory, it was a police state which ruled through terror tactics. We need also to remember that their magnificent buildings were constructed largely by slaves.

Outside the Gospels, there are few references to Jesus. The Jewish Historian, Josephus, includes a short paragraph about Jesus. However, our only record of what he wrote has come to us through Christian writers who edited Josephus' reference so much that he was made into a Christian. In the edited material, Josephus proclaims Jesus as the Messiah, who taught the truth and was resurrected after crucifixion. At the very least we know that Jesus was important enough to be mentioned by Josephus in his "Antiquities of the Jews."

Chapter 7

THE KINGDOM OF GOD

The kingdom of God is central in Jesus' teaching. Christians pray for the kingdom each time they pray the Lord's Prayer: *"Thy kingdom come, thy will be done on earth."* The kingdom of God is the rule of God: *"Thy will (rule) be done on earth, as it is in Heaven."* It is not a place or location on earth; rather, it is a way of life, when life is lived in the compassionate presence and under the generous guidance of the God Jesus knew so well. When an individual invites God to rule in his/her life, and labors to understand and follow the leading of God, then that person is living in the kingdom. When God rules "on earth" and the Caesars no longer rule, then the Lord's Prayer has finally been answered in its fullness. It is what the world would be like if God's ways were adopted and followed. It is a future expectation but can also be a personal experience in the present.

The kingdom of God is not a carefully practiced piety or the minute observance of a thoroughly studied religion, but a daily walk with God, living the life which reflects the ways and passion of the compassionate Heavenly Father. Such a one is in the kingdom of God, delighting in doing the Father's desires which are for the highest hopes of the human spirit. Jesus said, *"On that day many will say to me, 'Lord, Lord, did we not prophesy in your name, and cast out demons in your name, and do many deeds of power in your name?' Then I will declare to them, 'I never knew you; go away from me, you evildoers.'"* (Matt 7:22-23 NRSV). To Jesus, the goal of life is not to perform powerful ministries of service to humanity, as important as they are; it is being in communion with the living God, which leads inevitably to deeds of kindness in imitation of God whose blessings never cease and whose love is extended to all.

Some say the kingdom is something which only God will bring about, as implied in the Lord's Prayer where God is petitioned to establish the kingdom on earth, just as it is already in Heaven. While God may indeed do it, it is then a question of the process God chooses to follow. If it were all up to God, then Jesus would never have urged people to decide to enter the kingdom now by inviting God to rule in their personal lives. According to Mark, Jesus began his ministry with these words: *"The time has come,"* he said, *"the kingdom of God is near. Repent and believe the good news!"* (Mark 1:15). It is clearly implied that the kingdom of God is near, even present in Jesus' ministry. One time the Pharisees asked when the kingdom would come. Jesus replied, *"The kingdom of God does not come with your careful observation, nor will people say, 'Here it is,' or 'There it is,' because the kingdom of God is within you,"* (or among you). (Luke 17:20-21). When the individual accepts the authority of Jesus to pronounce the nearness of the kingdom and then invites the compassionate God of Jesus into his interior life, the kingdom has come in the present moment for that person.

If it is solely an action of God, then much of Jesus' teaching about the kingdom would need to be revised or eliminated. When he urged people not to be anxious about their needs, he said, *"Strive first for the kingdom of God and his righteousness, and all these things will be given to you as well."* (Matt 6:33). When he was accused of casting out demons by the power of Satan, he said, *"If I drive out demons by the Spirit of God, then the kingdom of God has come upon you."* (Matt 12:28). In both of these quotations, the kingdom of God can be experienced in the present moment.

As indicated, the kingdom of God was central in Jesus' teaching but, strangely, it does not appear as the central belief among the first Christians following the resurrection. They apparently believed Jesus would return soon and would then establish the kingdom on Earth. As Jesus' return did not happen as expected, the kingdom receded somewhat in importance, though the term "kingdom of God" was still used. The term occurs six times in the Book of Acts and eleven times in the epistles of Paul who almost always used it as a synonym for Heaven, perhaps because Paul was sure the end of the age and the return of Christ was about to happen. This is especially clear in his first letter to the Corinthian Christians where he writes that in the life to come, believers will not be housed in flesh and blood bodies: *"I declare to you, brothers, that flesh and blood cannot inherit the kingdom of God, nor does the perishable inherit the imperishable."* (1 Cor 15:50). In this passage, the kingdom is not a "flesh and blood" experience of this world. However, in his letter to the Romans, the great apostle seems to indicate that those who live in the Spirit are in the kingdom here and now: *"For the kingdom of God is not a matter of eating and drinking, but of righteousness, peace and joy in the Holy Spirit."* (Romans 14:17). To be in the Spirit is living in the will of God and that is living in the kingdom.

While the kingdom was the central theme of Jesus' teaching in the synoptic Gospels, it is almost completely missing in John. The term appears in John's gospel only twice, both times when Nicodemus visited Jesus at night in chapter three. How do we account for this difference?

The love of God for sinners constitutes the cornerstone of Jesus' message. He insisted that rituals and long-held beliefs and practices must give way in the present moment to his vision of the compassionate God. He told two parables which emphasize the need to decide now on entering the kingdom of God. The first is the parable of the great supper which comes to us in both Matthew and Luke. Matthew has changed his version to the extent that it almost misses the point entirely. Luke's parable is found in Luke 14:16f and may be summarized as follows: A man sets a date for a fine banquet and invites many friends. But when the day comes and he sends a servant to tell the invited guests that all is ready, each guest makes excuses why he cannot be present. In understandable anger, the host orders his servants to go out to the streets of the city and bring in the poor, blind, lame and maimed.

Still there is room for more, so the host sends his servants a second time to compel people to come in so that his house may be full. The parable ends with these words, *"I tell you, not one of those men who were invited will get a taste of my banquet."* (Luke 14:24). The poor, blind, lame and maimed do get to taste and enjoy the banquet.

In this parable Jesus was saying the time is now for his audience to enter God's kingdom rule. No excuses will be accepted. It is also a warning to those who believed they had God and religion thoroughly understood and practiced; they will fail to enter, while the poor, blind, lame and maimed will be gathered in by the compassionate God. Once again it is the amazing love of God for sinners which makes the difference. You may ask how the poor, blind, lame and maimed are sinners. The answer is that some people were convinced that if a person suffered from one of these troubles, it was because God was punishing him for some sin he had committed. Jesus knew better.

The second parable, which also emphasizes the need to make a decision in the present moment, is the story of the unjust steward found in Luke 16:1-9. A business man had a steward who was failing in his job and who was told by his employer to close out his accounts because he was fired. The steward has to do something quickly to avoid destitution. He decided to change the accounts in favor of those who owe his master money so that they might give him employment later. He wrongly reduces the debts of all those who owe his boss money. He felt he had to do something and do it now, which was the point of the parable: act in the present moment to enter God's kingdom by taking Jesus' message seriously.

Where did Jesus get his belief in the total goodness of God? When we put the evidence of Jesus' spiritual life together as found in the Gospels, we are led to conclude that his understanding of God came from his experience of God. It was not so much a theory about God or a vision of God, as it was a relationship Jesus had with God. It shows up clearly in the way he often addressed God as "Abba, Father." The Apostle Paul uses this word in his letter to the Galatians, *"Because you are children, God has sent the Spirit* of his Son into our hearts, crying, 'Abba, Father.'" (Gal 4:6 NRSV). Paul must have known that Jesus used the term "Abba" in his close relationship with the Heavenly Father. Jesus always referred to God as Father, and in the Lord's Prayer he taught his disciples to say "Our Father."

The Lord told two parables which clearly show the kingdom rule of God is a thing of great joy. He said, *"The kingdom of heaven is like treasure hidden in a field. When a man found it, he hid it again, and then in his joy went and sold all he had and bought that field."* (Matt 13:44). To be in the kingdom is to experience great joy. Note that Matthew uses kingdom of Heaven instead of kingdom of God. He was not referring to Heaven as the place where people go when they die. Matthew is the most Jewish of the Gospels, possibly written by a Jew. Like most Jews, Matthew did not want to use the word "God" more often than necessary. As a result, he writes of the kingdom of Heaven and not kingdom of God. Either way, letting God rule is like finding a treasure in a field.

The second parable is much like the first, *"Again, the kingdom of heaven is like a merchant in search of fine pearls; on finding one pearl of great value, he sold all that he had and bought it."* (Matt 13:45-46 RSV). This simple parable says that to possess the kingdom – to live in the kingdom rule of God - is to experience great joy; it is like finding a priceless pearl.

To repeat, the Pharisees once asked Jesus when the kingdom of God would come. Part of his answer was, *"the kingdom of God is within you."* The phrase "is within you," can also be translated "is among you." It is as close as the decision to daily invite God to rule in one's life, convinced that God's acceptance and love is so great that a person will want to live in the fellowship and compassion of God.

According to Luke's gospel the poor will always be welcome: *"Blessed are you who are poor, for yours is the kingdom of God."* (Luke 6:20 NRSV). The Greek word translated as "poor" in Luke's verse, "ptochos," is better translated not as "poor" but as "destitute." Jesus was saying the destitute are sure to enter the kingdom of God. Why? They are blessed because God knows what they are going through and is eager to welcome them into his eternal kingdom. Luke's verse does not apply to people who feel they are so heavily taxed they must put off for a year the purchase of a new and bigger yacht. Jesus did not hold out much hope for the wealthy, who are tempted to trust their money more than God: *"Again I tell you, it is easier for a camel to go through the eye of a needle than for a rich man to enter the kingdom of God."* (Matt 19:24).

Another group which will freely enter the kingdom are little children: *"'Let the little children come to me, and do not hinder them, for the kingdom of God belongs to such as these. I tell you the truth, anyone who will not receive the kingdom of God like a little child will never enter it.' And he took the children in his arms, put his hands on them and blessed them."* (Mark 10:14-16). The phrase, "such as these," includes adults who have the same trust and curiosity as a little child. It was people who were sure they had all the answers who posed the greatest hindrance to accepting Jesus' message.

The kingdom of God is living in that personal relationship which God longs for. It is God at home in the inmost being of the individual. It is being rather than doing. It is being a child of God, being in relationship with the living God. Jesus said in Matthew's Gospel, *"Truly I tell you, unless you change and become like children, you will never enter the kingdom of heaven."* (Matt 18:3 NRSV). As a child trusts and loves his mother and father and in that environment of full devotion grows and matures toward healthy adulthood, just so, the person who welcomes the love and ways of God will mature and grow. If we are uncertain about what the goodness of God looks like, we have only to consider Jesus, the Jesus who lived out his own union with God every day.

When Jesus blessed the little children, he certainly included little girls. He lived in an age when girls were not prized as much as boys. An ancient letter was found in the garbage dump of Oxyrhynchus, near Cairo, Egypt, written in the year 1BCE. It was written by a man named Hilarion to his wife, Alis, who was pregnant. He was working some distance from his home. The letter contains this sad order to Alis, his wife: "If by chance you bear a son, let it be. If it is a girl, throw it out." The girl would be thrown out to die, unless someone rescued it to bring it up as a slave.

Jesus was sure the kingdom was already present in his ministry to hurting people. He once answered his own question about the kingdom: *"What is the kingdom of God like? What shall I compare it to? It is like a mustard seed, which a man took and planted in his garden. It grew and became a tree, and the birds of the air perched in its branches."* (Luke 13:18-19). The mustard plant was a problem which farmers did not want in their gardens, since it grew so fast and could infest the whole garden. Jesus is saying the kingdom of God grows, it grows quickly and in time will cover the earth. This statement from Jesus argues against the belief that the kingdom will come only at the end of time. It is present and is growing now.

Some scholars do not agree with this interpretation because they believe Jesus always presented the kingdom as eschatological, which means it will come only at the end of the world when God acts to establish it. If that is true, then when Jesus began his ministry, according to Mark's gospel, why did he say, *"The time has come. The kingdom of God is near. Repent and believe the good news!"* (Mark 1:15). He was saying that the kingdom is open now to the person who is willing to welcome God's compassionate rule into his daily life. It is a day to day joyful determination to live God's way, and if sins are committed along the way, God understands and God's love continues. How great that God forgives, for Paul declares in Romans, *"All have sinned and fall short of the glory of God."* (Romans 3:23 RSV). Jesus' message was: "God loves sinners," and he demonstrated his belief by daily associating with people some liked to call "sinners" and "outcasts."

The kingdom exists on the personal level when the individual is convinced that God can be trusted fully, with the result that he or she makes the decision to welcome God and God's compassionate rule into the interior realm of devotion and life. It begins with the initial opening of the heart and mind to the living God. It continues and grows as it is consciously renewed and experienced at select times during the day and in caught moments of heightened spiritual awareness. It is not giving consent to a doctrine about God; it is the firsthand experience of God, an experience which is based on the certainty that God is the source of joy, love, meaning and hope. God is all those things we value most, and more. It is enjoying the God-reality we are immersed in every waking hour, based on the certainty that the God of Jesus is welcoming, compassionate and accepting. The kingdom of God is rightly interpreted as the rule of God, but it was never presented by Jesus as obeying the rules of God. Instead, it is entering into the very heart of God, for *"God is love."* (1 John 4:8). Communion with God is found not only in the experience of joy and celebration, but even in sorrow, suffering and grief.

Living in the kingdom is a continuing conversation with the God who communicates by often speaking to us in the sound of silence. It is looking for and experiencing God in children, people, and nature. It is singing without sound, a song of thanksgiving when blessings are identified by day or by night. It is seeing the world differently, like the poet who was in the kingdom when he wrote: *"The heavens declare the glory of God; the skies proclaim the work of his hands. Day after day they pour out speech; night after night they display knowledge."* (Psalm19:1-2). God communicates in countless ways, even when we are concentrating on our work, while part of us is still listening. It is living with the firm conviction that life has purpose even when we cannot see any meaning. It is trusting God's vision more than we trust our own. We learn God's vision from the living Jesus.

It was Jesus' intention that the kingdom of God was to be embraced by individuals who were willing to receive the Spirit with the maximum surrender and devotion, which leads to life-changing results. This can be seen in many teachings. In Matthew 6:5 he told his hearers that prayer is not for show, but for communion with God, though he did not use that term. *"Go into your room and shut the door and pray to your Father who is in secret."* Instead of worrying oneself and God about life's necessities, Jesus urged people to trust God instead and strive for the life-giving, communion-rule of the Father. He said, *"Seek first his kingdom and his righteousness, and all these things will be given you as well,"* (Matt 6:33). Jesus could encourage people to seek first God's kingdom because he knew it was possible to experience the compassionate rule of God in the present moment. He experienced it in his own life. He told the crowd that God is much more concerned for their needs than any human father: *"If you, then, though you are evil, (*human*), know how to give good gifts to your children, how much more will your Father in heaven give good gifts to those who ask him!"* (Matthew 7:11 RSV).

Some scholars are convinced that Jesus' teaching about the kingdom applied only to a future time. Others believe Jesus was certain the kingdom would be established in his day or in the lifetime of his disciples. Although it is in apocalyptic material and may not be trustworthy, Jesus is recorded as saying: *"I tell you the truth, this generation will certainly not pass away until all these things have happened."* (Matt 24:34). Did this statement truly come from Jesus before his crucifixion, or does it reflect more accurately the church when Matthew's gospel was written? That church may have believed the statement came from the living Christ who may have spoken to them through the Spirit.

Some speculate that Jesus believed God would act to inaugurate the kingdom when he went to Jerusalem for the Passover and that he still believed it right up to the crucifixion. If Jesus' prayer in the Garden of Gethsemane is historical, he believed God could act to save him and his kingdom message, but he was still willing to accept disaster and death if God allowed it. But how do we know what he prayed in the Garden, since it took place away from the disciples who were sleeping? We wish we had more information. Nevertheless, we know what did happen and we must deal with the fact that God did not intervene. It appears that Jesus finally yielded to despair when he uttered the cry of dereliction as he hung in agony on the cross: *"At three o'clock Jesus cried out with a loud voice, 'Eloi, Eloi, lemasabachthani?'*

which means, 'My God, my God, why have you forsaken me?'"
(Mark 15:34 NRSV). Jesus' cry came from Psalm 22, which begins
with the same words Jesus uttered as he died.

Jesus saw himself as the agent of God called to proclaim and
demonstrate the good news of God's radical love. This enabled
him to say, *"Whoever welcomes me welcomes the one who sent
me."* (Matt 10:40 NRSV). His audience needed confidence in him
as God's spokesman in order to regard his message as valid. But
his message was also communicated when people observed how he
freely associated with all kinds of people, especially those who
were shunned and rejected by others. It was a visible
demonstration of his acceptance of all people, and a reminder of
God's acceptance. This was his mission, to proclaim the kingdom
of God as a relationship of individuals to the God of infinite love
and compassion. The only requirement, in the total democracy of
God's kingdom, was to live in the certainty of one's personal
acceptance by God and God's acceptance of all others. It was
radical in its inclusiveness, and its democracy. Acceptance in the
kingdom did not in any way depend on how faithfully one kept the
Law or made frequent sacrifices in the Temple or regularly
repented of one's failures. Jesus never mentioned such
requirements. Jesus was certain they were all loved, cherished and
valued by the Heavenly Father. All a person needed to do was
accept God's amazing love for him/her as an individual, and God's
compassion for all others.

The reader might rightly ask about the apocalyptic or "end of
the world" material found in Matthew 24:4-36, Mark 13:5-37 and
Luke 21:8-36. Not only is it there, but Jesus is presented as
speaking at length about it in answer to a question from the
disciples: *"Tell us, when will these things happen? And what will
be the sign that they are all about to be fulfilled?"* (Mark 13:4).
The disciples were impressed with the massive stones in the
Temple structure, some weighing sixty tons. Jesus prophesied that
the time was coming when not one stone would be left on top of
another. He could see that his people would someday rebel against
Roman rule and be crushed. The Zealots were talking about it all

the time. The disciples wanted to know when these massive stones would be destroyed, which marks the beginning of the apocalyptic material in which Jesus is reported to have made many statements about the end of the world.

There are many good Christians who are as fascinated as the disciples with this type of thinking and writing and tend to exalt it above most everything else Jesus said. Most main line scholars are convinced that much of this material was already available in Jewish literature and thinking. Enough early Christians were attracted to it, and repeated it, so that it was eventually regarded as coming from Jesus. The author is convinced that little, if any, of this material came from Jesus, but was circulating in the church which existed at the time the gospels were written. Among Jesus' own people, there was some interest in the "end time," although many of his people put all their emphasis on this life, with relatively little thought about what might happen after death or the consummation of all things at the end of time. Too many of Jesus' people were chiefly concerned with what they were going to eat today and tomorrow.

In the apocalyptic verses, Jesus is reported as saying that many will come in his name claiming to be the Messiah, there will be wars and rumors of wars, nations will rise up against nations, there will be famines, earthquakes and plagues, and Christians will be severely persecuted. All of these sad events have happened many times in the past and some are happening in modern times. Luke has Jesus contradict himself by saying: *They will put some of you to death. But not a hair of your head will perish. By standing firm you will gain life."* (Luke 21:16-19). Luke adds some genuine history when he has Jesus speak of the Jewish rebellion against Rome in which they were totally defeated, with Jerusalem and the Temple destroyed: *"When you see Jerusalem being surrounded by armies, you will know that its desolation is near. Then let those who are in Judea flee to the mountains, let those in the city get out, and let those in the country not enter the city."* (Luke 21:20-21). We remember that both Matthew and Luke were written long after Jerusalem and the Temple were destroyed by the Romans in 70

CE. All three Gospels give the same ending to the apocalyptic additions using almost the same words: *"I tell you the truth, this generation will certainly not pass away until all these things have happened."* (Mark 13:30). But just two verses later, Mark has Jesus say, *"No one knows about that day or hour, not even the angels in heaven, nor the Son, but only the Father."* (Mark 13:32). This verse sounds like it came from Jesus, but so much of the apocalyptic material does not. The question remains: why are so many Christians attracted to "end of the world" speculations? Does it give these good people a sense of power over current events which they feel are not going in the "right" direction? How much better it is to simply trust God and faithfully follow Jesus, whose great passion was for the poor, sick, disabled, ignored and condemned, no matter what this may do to one's politics.

The apocalyptic material is a strong mixture of fear and faith on the part of Christians who faced persecution and who longed for the return of the Savior and who were trying desperately to find direction and comfort, sometimes in questionable beliefs. Since Jesus said only God knows about these things, the best course of action is to let God take care of it. When we do that, we are in the kingdom of God by allowing God to rule.

While the apocalyptic material presents problems, most scholars are convinced that Jesus believed that God's world-wide rule will come at some future time, determined only by God. Meanwhile, it is possible to allow God to rule here and now, in the same way Jesus experienced the Heavenly Father, with full trust and confidence.

Some scholars believe Jesus went to his death still believing that the kingdom of God was about to be established. Instead of the kingdom, God gave resurrection. As a result, the disciples came together in Jerusalem to await Jesus' soon return when they thought he would fully establish the kingdom on earth. We are still waiting, still trusting and still working, following Jesus

Chapter 8

THE TEACHING OF JESUS

Jesus was frequently addressed as Rabbi, the Jewish word for Teacher. In the next paragraphs we get a sampling of his skill as a teacher of moral and religious truth. The most important feature of Jesus' teaching is his central emphasis on the superlative love of God for all people, especially those at the bottom of religion and society, the outcasts, sinners, tax collectors and prostitutes.

It is easy to say that the compassion of God is seen in God's forgiveness of sinners. But Jesus' Gospel is much better than that. To Jesus, God's forgiveness does not come after repentance; it comes before a person repents and is not dependent on one's desire to be forgiven. To Jesus, each individual is a child of God and the Heavenly Father loves his children with a love which goes far beyond the love of human parents for their children. In Luke's gospel Jesus says: *"If you then, though you are evil, know how to give good gifts to your children, how much more will your Father in heaven give the Holy Spirit to those who ask him."* (Luke 11:13). We have already quoted the same passage from Matthew with the exception that Luke says the Father gives the Holy Spirit to those who ask him, while Matthew says God gives "good gifts" to those who ask him. Good parents love their children long before the child has done anything to merit their sacrificial love. Jesus said God's love is like that of caring parents, only much greater. God's love comes before everything. Even though there may be nothing in a person which merits God's love, neither is there anything which can stop it. God's love cannot be earned; it is given to everyone.

Because the forgiveness of God is freely given to all, Jesus demanded that each individual must imitate the Heavenly Father and freely forgive others when they are injured by them. *"If you forgive men when they sin against you, your heavenly Father will also forgive you. But if you do not forgive men their sins, your Father will not forgive your sins."* (Matt 6:14-15). Failure to forgive others is the only time God's forgiveness is withheld, perhaps because the one who does not forgive others, may not feel any need to be forgiven and will never ask for it. But Jesus says God is still "your Father." The same idea is found in Jesus' comment on judging others. *"Do not judge, or you too will be judged. For in the same way you judge others, you will be judged."* (Matt 7:1-2). This is true, not only in one's relationship with God, but in one's popularity with others. The judgmental person is often shunned and treated as undesirable.

Jesus taught that God's compassion is so abundant that the trusting person can be sure that every need can be presented to the Heavenly Father. *"Ask, and it will be given you; seek, and you will find; knock, and it will be opened to you. For everyone who asks receives, and he who seeks finds, and to him who knocks it will be opened."* (Luke 11:9-11). This statement may prompt us to apply it to unanswered prayer. How do we cope with the seeming silence of God when we have fervently prayed for a personal need or for a child or a friend and our petitions are not granted? It helps to remember the prayer of Jesus in Gethsemane when he asked that the cup of suffering and death be taken from him. He ended by saying *"Not my will, but yours be done."* If Jesus had been spared and went on to live a normal life, we probably would know nothing about him. Meanwhile, the best way to live is in constant, expectant faith, that faith which finds, receives and for whom doors are opened. There is no doubt Jesus believed that no matter what happens, we are on the winning side with God.

Jesus was criticized for eating with tax collectors and sinners. He said to his opponents, *"It is not the healthy who need a doctor, but the sick. I have not come to call the righteous, but sinners."* (Mark 2:17). He was not only concerned for tax collectors and sinners but also for the sick and troubled, a concern he made abundantly clear came from God. And although they would not admit it, his concern also included his critics and enemies.

Jesus believed God's love goes far beyond the forgiveness of sinners; it goes to God's radical love for sinners. It is not that God's love swings into action when the sinner turns to God in repentance; it is rather the sinner turns to God when he realizes how much God cares for him, and had cared for him all along. Jesus wanted people to know that in all of one's past and in the "now" moment, the love of God is given. Jesus' compassionate desire was to free the sick and the troubled from the futile search for the right way to please God so that their sickness and pain could be relieved. Jesus knew God was not punishing them for some sin they had committed.

It is a sad mistake to limit Jesus' teaching to an ethical and moral program. It is much greater and more important than that. To Jesus, every moral code is of little help compared to the imitation of God whose compassion and acceptance is totally trustworthy, allowing the believer to move forward in hope toward a more confident understanding of life in the physical world. The Lord taught people to care for others, convinced of the goodness of God, ready to imitate God in all relationships, allowing love for others to flow freely. One of the greatest human needs is the need to be forgiven, for to be human is to forget, to fail, to be selfish, to sin. Jesus made it abundantly clear that God understands this, but still loves people. God loves humans; all humans. Since this is true, it means we live in a world which is good and favors life and joy. This is true in spite of the horrible and unbelievable atrocities which humans have inflicted on one another. The world needs Jesus and his Good News.

Jesus had to face the problem of Biblical interpretation. He distinguished between the important and the unimportant in the Jewish Scripture. In Mark, he modified the clean and unclean food laws: *"Nothing outside a man can make him unclean by going into him. Rather, it is what comes out of a man that makes him unclean."* (Mark 7:15). He explained the difference to his disciples: *"From within, out of men's hearts, come evil thoughts, sexual immorality, theft, murder, adultery, greed, malice, deceit, lewdness, envy, slander, arrogance and folly. All these evils come from inside and make a man 'unclean.'"* (Mark 7:21-23).

He rated ceremonial laws low and ethical laws high. When the disciples were criticized for pulling wheat grains off the stalk on the Sabbath, Jesus said, *"The Sabbath was made for man, not man for the Sabbath."* (Mark 2:27 RSV). Human need was above ritual requirements, which is why he felt free to heal the sick on the Sabbath. He said God prefers mercy not sacrifice, quoting Hosea 6:6.

In Matthew, he set aside the Law of retaliation which demanded *"an eye for an eye and a tooth for a tooth."* (Exodus 21:23 RSV). Instead of hitting back, he said, *"I tell you, do not resist an evil person. If someone strikes you on the right cheek, turn to him the other also. And if someone wants to sue you and take your tunic, let him have your cloak as well. If someone forces you to go one mile, go with him two miles."* (Matt 5:39-41). This has been difficult for many good Christians. Where it has been tried, it has often worked to soften the hard and angry heart, whereas retaliations have often erupted in terrible strife and even wars.

Jesus' belief in the compassion of God did not come from any theory; it came from his experience of God. He knew God was compassionate, welcoming and encouraging, quick to accept people the way they were, not demanding repentance or a radical change of life before God's embrace was given. He told numerous parables that clearly portray his vision of God. Here is one as recorded in the Gospel of Luke: *"Two men went up to the temple to pray, one a Pharisee and the other a tax collector. The Pharisee stood up and prayed about himself: 'God, I thank you that I am not like other men – robbers, evildoers, adulterers – or even like this tax collector. I fast twice a week and give a tenth of all I get.' But the tax collector stood at a distance. He would not even look up to heaven, but beat his breast and said, 'God, have mercy on me, a sinner.'"* Jesus said, *"I tell you that this man* (the tax collector) *rather than the other* (the Pharisee) *went home justified before*

God. For everyone who exalts himself will be humbled, and he who humbles himself will be exalted." (Luke 18:10-14 RSV). To most Pharisees, a tax collector was at the opposite pole from a hard-striving Pharisee. As pointed out earlier, a tax collector was a Jew hired by the Romans to collect the Roman tax. While they were hated by most of their countrymen, Jesus said in this parable the tax collector was justified by God, not the self-righteous Pharisee. The parable clearly reveals Jesus' portrayal of God as compassionate and accepting even of those who appear to be on the wrong side such as tax collectors.

Jesus clearly taught that God directs his blessings to all people, the good and the bad equally. In Matthew, Jesus encouraged his audience to love their enemies so that *"you may be sons of your Father in heaven. He causes his sun to rise on the evil and the good, and sends rain on the righteous and the unrighteous."* (Matt 5:45). In other words, it is not possible to walk down a street on a sunny day and find that the sun does not shine on the homes of evil people, only on the homes of the good people. Neither is it possible to drive down a street on a rainy day, with rain falling everywhere except on just one house which never gets any rain and where nothing can grow, all because very bad people live there. Jesus concluded this passage by saying, *"Be perfect, therefore, as your heavenly Father is perfect"* (Matt 5:48 NRSV). Luke's version of the same incident may have a better conclusion: "Be merciful, even as your Father is merciful." (Luke 6:36 RSV). Even closer to the thinking of Jesus is: Be compassionate, even as your Father is compassionate.

However, in each version, Jesus is encouraging people to be like God. Jesus' fundamental belief was that God is compassionate, merciful, accepting, encouraging and certainly forgiving, without requiring repentance first. He believed that when people know they are accepted, loved and valued by God, they will want to do God's will and make personal improvements in the direction of becoming more like the God of preeminent love, the God Jesus knew. According to Jesus, God has a more hopeful, positive and encouraging attitude toward people than people do who often emphasize the weaknesses and failures of other humans. Jesus spoke of the Heavenly Father who looks on humans as his children who need and who always have his love and encouragement.

Jesus made the extravagant love of God perfectly clear in the fifteenth chapter of Luke's gospel which contains three parables of lost things: the lost sheep, the lost coin and the lost boy, better known as the parable of the prodigal son. All three of these parables say something great about God, who is like the good shepherd, who will not stop looking until he has found his lost sheep; and who is like the housewife who will not stop looking until she finds her lost coin; and who is like the father who patiently waits for his son to come back home after setting out to make a way for himself in the world and who failed miserably. Jesus told these parables to say something amazing about God.

Matthew also contains the story of the lost sheep, although there is a significant difference between Matthew's account and Luke's. Luke emphasizes repentance while Matthew does not. Luke adds, *"I tell you that in the same way there will be more rejoicing in heaven over one sinner who repents than over ninety-nine righteous persons who do not need to repent."* (Luke 15:7). Luke includes this same expression at the end of the parable of the lost coin. Luke is thinking of people, since neither sheep nor coins are capable of repentance. Luke emphasizes repentance in his gospel more than is found in the Gospels of Matthew and Mark. We might also ask, how many righteous persons are there "who do not need to repent"?

Let us review these three parables in greater detail. Jesus said a shepherd had 100 sheep. One strayed away and was lost. The shepherd secured the 99 sheep and went looking for the one that was lost. He does not stop looking until he finds the wandering sheep which he carries back to rejoin the 99. When he is with the other shepherds he says, *"Rejoice with me; I have found my lost sheep."* Luke adds, *"I tell you that in the same way there will be more rejoicing in heaven over one sinner who repents than over ninety-nine righteous persons who do not need to repent."* (Luke 15:6-7). Jesus did not tell this story to inform his audience what a shepherd does when a sheep gets lost. They already knew that. He told the parable to help his hearers understand that God never gives up on a single child of his when it strays and is lost. And when God recovers the lost boy or girl, man or woman, there is a joyful celebration.

The second parable is of a woman who has ten silver coins, but one day discovers that one coin is missing. She sweeps the house until she finds the lost coin. She goes to her neighbors and invites them to rejoice with her because her coin has been found. Once again, there is celebration, just as there was when the lost sheep was found. There are two features of this story which are worthy of notice. First, the woman is not God, just as the shepherd is not God, but from the woman and the shepherd we learn something about God, which is why Jesus told the parables. The second feature has to do with the difference between a sheep and a coin. A sheep has legs and can easily wander away and get lost; coins cannot get lost on their own. It was not the coin's fault that it was lost. We can be reasonably sure Jesus did not include this in his parable, but it is still true, that there are many children and adults who get lost, though it is not their fault. A boy or girl may have a very abusive family life plus nearly insurmountable growing-up challenges, getting into trouble and going in and out of jail. But is it really their fault? The scripture says we are to be our brother's keeper. If society, especially the church, does not care about home life, school quality, neighborhood environment, then maybe we need to rethink Jesus' parable about the coin. Don't you think Jesus would say, "It's not their fault"?

The most important of these three parables is the parable of the prodigal son, which is sometimes called the parable of the two brothers. The younger son is bold enough to demand the inheritance that will come to him following the custom of the time regarding a younger son. The oldest son gets the farm and the bulk of the inheritance. But a younger son usually got a sum of money which would enable him to strike out on his own and make a life for himself. In this case the young son is rather immature; he wants to see the world; he wants to discover what lies beyond the next mountain. But he does not know how to control his appetites. Very soon after he leaves home, all the inheritance money is gone and the only job this Jewish boy can find is feeding a Gentile farmer's pigs. Many of the Jews of that time would say the boy is no longer a Jew. Feeding swine would make him a Jew who had become a Gentile and was no longer welcome in the community.

The prodigal is tempted to eat the slop which he feeds to the hogs, so great is his hunger. In desperation he decides to go home in the hope that his father will have mercy and take him back as a hired servant, so that he will have food to eat and a place to sleep. Meanwhile, his father, (probably with the boy's mother), no doubt went out to a high point every day where they could see if anyone was traveling up the distant valley road. The day finally comes when they see a solitary figure in the distance and it looks like it could be their son. As the traveler comes nearer, they see that it is their boy. When near enough, the father can see his son is in rags, he has no sandals on his feet and no ring on his finger. That missing ring signified that he was his father's son, but now it is gone.

What does the father do when he sees the condition of his son? Some in Jesus' audience were probably thinking the father should shout at his son, "Don't think of stopping here boy; you just keep on going, you don't belong here anymore." But the father does not wait for the prodigal to come to him; instead he runs to his son, embraces him and kisses him. Note that nothing is said about the inheritance money. Rather, the father begins to issue urgent orders to his hired servants. One is to find the best robe in the house and put it on him. Another is to locate a fine ring and put it on his finger and still another servant is charged with finding sandals for his blistered feet. The father doesn't say a word about the money or why his son was dressed in rags. He takes him back, not as a hired servant, but as his son who has come home at last. A sumptuous banquet is ordered for a great celebration.

As already pointed out, Jesus deliberately told this parable and the other two to show what God is like. He was saying that God is like that father who waits patiently for his child's return and when he does return, no questions are asked; there is only embrace and celebration. That is the nature of God who celebrates when his wandering child comes home. Remember: the word repent in the Bible contains the idea of return. This parable is different from the story of the shepherd who was able to go looking for the lost sheep, and the housewife, who is also able to look for the lost coin, for the father could not go over the hills looking for his son. The father can only wait, as the Heavenly Father must wait until the shipwrecked soul responds to the urgings of the Spirit and in desperation tries Jesus and his good news of the compassionate God. According to the Epistle of First John, *"God is love."* (1 John 4:8 RSV). We are grateful to John for that invaluable insight; for God is not only love but joy, and hope, and celebration, and every positive value and experience we long for. When we love, we are participating in the very being of God. The same is true when we are joyful.

Earlier it was noted the parable of the prodigal son could also be named the parable of two brothers, for the elder brother now comes on the scene. He is upset and angry and he has a legitimate complaint. Why did no one go into the fields where he was working to tell him his brother had come home and there was going to be a great celebration? He had to find it out for himself when he heard the music and singing. It was probably a servant who told him his brother had come home and the father has ordered a banquet to celebrate. We imagine someone also told him about the younger brother's condition which only adds to the older brother's rising anger. When his father comes out to encourage him to be part of the celebration, he reminded his dad that his young son had no doubt spent his money on prostitutes. He adds that in all the years he has labored for his father, his dad never gave him even a little lamb to have a party with his friends. The father understands, but reminds him that everything he has is his, but his wayward brother was the same as dead, but has now come back to life; he was lost but now is found.

It is probably true that some of the people who heard Jesus give this parable mentally sided with the older brother. The same people also would have felt there is no way the father's forgiveness of his son says anything about God. But the outcasts, sinners, tax collectors and prostitutes who heard the parable would have identified with the prodigal son and would have gone away with a little more hope and a little more confidence in their acceptance by God and their place in God's affection.

Jesus tried to convince people to change their attitude toward the things they worried about, including food, clothing and life itself, by trusting God for everything. He said, *"Your heavenly Father knows that you need them. But seek first his kingdom and his righteousness, and all these things will be given to you as well."* (Matt 6:32-33 NRSV). More important than securing the necessities of life is being under God's kingdom rule, for the Heavenly Father wants his children to have all they need. Jesus felt the greatest need was for God.

The great invitation in Matthew 11 is often quoted as providing comfort for those who are overloaded with cares. It is more than that. It is a call from the Lord to take up the task of understanding and embracing his message of God's love: *"Come to me, all you that are weary and are carrying heavy burdens and I will give you rest. Take my yoke upon you, and learn from me; for I am gentle and humble in heart, and you will find rest for your souls. For my yoke is easy, and my burden is light."* (Matt 11:28-30 NRSV).

He knew it was not easy for many of his listeners, especially his critics, to understand and embrace his message, which required hard work, as the above quotation reveals. The yoke he spoke of was the leather or wooden collar which was slipped over the neck of a horse or ox, which was then fastened by use of ropes or chains to a plow or a wagon so the animal's strength could be put to work. A yoke was a symbol of hard work. Jesus knew how greatly his audience was weighed down by unhelpful religious convictions. To break through to new understandings required an effort. For some, it was entirely too much. They were not willing to do the hard work of reexamining their religious practices, which served to keep them boxed in.

The caring God knows our needs and responds in a proactive

way when we put God's caring ways at the center of personal living. Some of Jesus' parables were a warning against preconceived ideas, blinding people to the liberating challenge in his good news.

A saying of Jesus which warns against pre-determined ideas and practices is found in his description of the Pharisees and the Scribes. He said: *"They are like children sitting in the marketplace and calling out to each other: 'We played the flute for you, and you did not dance; we sang a dirge, and you did not cry.'"* (Luke 7:32). Jesus then added, *"John the Baptist came eating no bread and drinking no wine; and you say, 'He has a demon.' The Son of man,* (Jesus), *has come eating and drinking; and you say, 'Behold, a glutton and a drunkard, a friend of tax collectors and sinners!'"* (Luke 7:33-34). Jesus saw his message was up against the same reception which one group of children in the market was having as they tried to get another group of children to respond to their invitations to play a game; they would not dance and they would not cry. In the same way, the Pharisees refused to respond to Jesus' message; no matter how Jesus tried, they would neither dance nor cry.

He then enlarged on how the closed minds of his critics not only prevented them from responding to his message but also to the message of John the Baptist. Neither Jesus nor John was good enough for them. They were correct when they accused Jesus of being "a friend of tax collectors and sinners." Not only did Jesus teach acceptance of "sinners and outcasts," he demonstrated his teaching by personally including them in his table fellowship. He may have eaten with them daily, which is why his critics called him a glutton. Jesus practiced radical equality in which everyone is included, and he made it clear the Heavenly Father does the same. His critics were sure they already knew the mind of God and in their opinion Jesus' mistake was failing to know who was to be excluded and condemned.

A scribe asked Jesus what was the greatest commandment, to which he replied, "*'You shall love the Lord your God with all your heart, and with all your soul, and with all your mind, and with all your strength.' The second is this, 'You shall love your neighbor as yourself.' There is no other commandment greater than these."* (Mark 12:30-31 RSV). This was a quotation from Deuteronomy 6:4-5 which faithful Jews repeated twice each day. But how can a person love God so completely? It is certainly a worthy goal, but perfection is surely beyond the ability of mortals. Jesus understood this and that is why he taught that God's acceptance and love comes first and does not depend on one's performance.

We have already looked at Matthew's account of how Jesus compared human parental love to God's love. The following gives Luke's account of this same comparison: *"If you then, though you are evil,* (human*) know how to give good gifts to your children, how much more will your Father in heaven give the Holy Spirit to those who ask him!"* (Luke 11:13). For Luke, God's ultimate gift is the Holy Spirit. Since true parents love their child before the child can do anything to merit that love, Jesus believed that God's love, which is greater, is given before any good or bad behavior and continues on. This was not just a theory for Jesus; it grew out of his own experience of God.

Another strong argument in favor of the generosity and kindness Jesus found in God is the disturbing parable of the laborers in the vineyard. He said a wealthy vineyard owner hired some laborers at 6 a.m. to work a twelve hour day for one denarius. The owner continued to hire groups of workers as he found them in the town square at different times of the day. The last group worked only one hour, while the first group worked 12 hours through the heat of the day. Yet when it came time to pay the workers, the owner paid all of them the same amount - one denarius. Those who had worked all day, complained to the owner who said to them, *"Friend, I am not being unfair to you. Didn't you agree to work for a denarius? Take your pay and go. I want to give the man who was hired last the same as I gave you. Don't I have the right to do what I want with my own money? Or are you upset because I am generous?"* (Matt 20:13-15).

This has always been a difficult parable for many Christians. It seems to be a surefire way to generate trouble with one's employees. The parable has nothing to do with labor relations. It is all about God, who can accept anyone God wants to, even eleventh hour people who all their lives were on the wrong side of morality, ethics and goodness. God accepts sinners, not just the good sinners, but all sinners. Jesus must have learned this from his prayerful meditations with God.

In both Matthew and Luke, Jesus included Gentiles in the Kingdom. In Luke Jesus says, *"People will come from east and west and north and south, and will take their places at the feast in the kingdom of God."* (Luke 13:28). In the previous verse he says some of his antagonists will weep when they see *"Abraham, Isaac and Jacob and all the prophets in the kingdom of God, but you yourselves thrown out."* (Luke 13:28). While the mission to the whole world developed after the resurrection, it grew out of these earlier statements by Jesus. The only people who may not enter the kingdom are those who are sure they are meeting all the requirements and are certain nothing can keep them out. They believed they were already in God's kingdom rule.

There is a helpful development in the Bible in the idea of God, sin and its cure and hope for this life and whatever lies beyond. Those who see development almost always see Jesus as providing the best revelation of God the Bible has to offer. Jesus believed in, served and loved the "Abba, Father" whose love for his many children begins and continues without any pre-conditions. God's only demand is the demand which love commands.

There are some sayings attributed to Jesus which he may not have spoken, at least not in their present form. Consider the parable Jesus may have told of the Unmerciful Servant. It ends with these words: *"In anger his master turned him over to the jailers to be tortured, until he should pay back all he owed. This is how my heavenly Father will treat each of you unless you forgive your brother from your heart."* (Matt 18:34-35). This is from Matthew which we have seen has a strong tendency to be harshly judgmental.

Jesus told the story in answer to Peter's question about how often he was required to forgive when a brother sinned against him. In the story, a servant owed his master a huge debt which his master agreed to forgive. But the servant went out and found a man who owed him a small amount and had him thrown in jail until he paid the debt. When the master of the forgiven servant learned of what he had done to the man who owed him a small sum, the master reversed his judgment and had the unforgiving servant imprisoned to be tortured until he somehow paid his enormous debt. It is the closing words which are especially shocking: *"This is how my heavenly Father will treat each of you unless you forgive your brother from your heart."* (Matt 18:35). We can be sure that was Matthew speaking and not Jesus. We take note that it was not Jewish practice to allow a debtor to be tortured until the debt was paid. This too, sounds like it probably came from the time when the Gospel of Matthew was written, about 50 or more years after the time Jesus gave the parable.

Mark includes a saying which has a strong note of judgment, but still could have come from Jesus, *"If anyone causes one of these little ones who believe in me to sin, it would be better for him to be thrown into the sea with a large millstone tied around his neck."* (Mark 9:42). It is a strong statement on the absolute need for children to be protected and cared for.

Do you think Jesus could have spoken the following: *"The Son of Man will send out his angels, and they will weed out of his kingdom everything that causes sin and all who do evil. They will throw them into the fiery furnace, where there will be weeping and gnashing of teeth."* (Matt 13:41-42).This comes from the apocalyptic material found in all three of the synoptic gospels. It deals with the end of the world when some people believed terrifying events would take place, followed by the judgment. It is doubtful if many authentic words of Jesus are found in apocalyptic writing found in the gospels, unless the following came from Jesus, as recorded in both Matthew and Mark, *"No one knows about that day or hour, not even the angels in heaven, nor the Son, but only the Father."* (Mark 13:30,32). Since these words no doubt came from Jesus, it is obvious he felt "end of the world" issues should be left in the hands of God. Even so, there are many popular preachers who are sure they have the "end times" completely understood often to the very day and hour.

In the 23rd chapter of Matthew, Jesus has some amazingly sharp words directed at the Scribes and Pharisees. But did these words truly come from Jesus? In this chapter he calls them, "hypocrites, blind guides, blind fools, whitewashed tombs, full of hypocrisy and lawlessness, snakes and brood of vipers." These are all terms which John the Baptist aimed at those who came to hear him preach on the banks of the Jordan River. Are they John's words which Matthew mistakenly attributed to Jesus? They do not sound at all like Jesus. To attack one's opponents with such vicious language would surely result in anger and retaliation. Anyone attacked in such a manner will not want to examine his practices with a view to making improvements. Instead, he will resolve to fight back with every weapon at his disposal. Were any Pharisees present when Jesus said to his audience, *"You are the light of the world. Let your light shine before others, so that they may see your good works and give glory to your Father in heaven?"* (Matt 5:14,16 NRSV). These words from Jesus, not the others, might invite even a proud Pharisee to wonder if his doctrines might be modified to produce a little more light and glory to God. We also know there were some Pharisees who were attracted to Jesus, and the Pharisees, as a group, represented the highest social development among the Jews of Jesus' day. How could Jesus descend into name calling?

If these words were not originally those of John the Baptizer, then they might have originated during that early time in the history of the church when Christians were all Jewish and fully convinced that Jesus was the Messiah. They were enthusiastically sharing their belief with Jewish neighbors. But it is clear that their neighbors were sometimes hostile and unreceptive. The leader of the Jewish Christians in Jerusalem was James, the brother of Jesus. He was eventually executed and became one of the first Christian martyrs. The Apostle Paul may have entered the story at about this time, since he tells us that he persecuted Jewish Christians in and around Jerusalem before his conversion. It was on the way to

Damascus to arrest more Christians that Paul had an amazing experience and was converted to Jesus as the Messiah. When the above is analyzed, it seems more possible the attacks against the scribes and Pharisees in Matthew 23 originated among the Jewish Christians in Palestine and did not come from Jesus.

At least one of the parables has a summary ending which tends to betray the reason why the parable was used. Consider the parable of the last judgment found in Matthew 25:31-46. The parable is not found in the other gospels. Scholars are often skeptical about a parable or event which is found in only one gospel. It has another strike against it because it is included in the apocalyptic material which has to do with the end of the world and the final judgment. The parable begins with the Son of Man coming to earth with all the angels to judge the nations, separating people as though they were sheep and goats. The sheep are good and go on the right hand, while the goats are evil and go on the left hand. Note that even before the sheep or goats are examined, they are judged to be either good or evil. It is very possible that Jesus may have spoken a parable like this, but by the time it passed through the memories of Christians before it was finally written down, it picked up a strong content of judgment. Does it sound like Jesus to say that some people are pre-judged as cursed and deserving of eternal punishment? That came from Matthew and the group of Christians he was part of when he wrote his Gospel. It did not come from Jesus.

The greatest difficulty Jesus faced in his teaching was in getting people to break loose from traditional conclusions about God and God's will for them, enabling them to see God, themselves and others in a better and more compassionate light. Once he said: *"If the light (understanding) in you is darkness, how great is the darkness,"* (Matthew 6:22.23 RSV) He was saying "if your thinking is not liberated and open to new truth, you are in darkness, even though you think you have the light of true knowledge."

There were some in his day, just as there are in ours, who put too much emphasis on money, or the lack of money. He tried to change their thinking by saying, *"No one can serve two masters. Either he will hate the one and love the other, or he will be devoted to the one and despise the other. You cannot serve both God and money,"* (Matt 6:24). He said some alarming words about the rich, who will have trouble getting into the kingdom of God because they trust more in their money than in God. He said, *"How hard it is for the rich to enter the kingdom of God! It is easier for a camel to go through the eye of a needle than for a rich man to enter the kingdom of God."* (Mark 10:25). He also said, *"But woe to you who are rich, for you have already received your comfort.* (Luke 6:24). In Luke 12:16, he told the parable of the rich man who built bigger barns to store his crops so he could retire in luxury, only to die that night. In Luke 16:19, he told of the rich man who feasted every day, never paying any attention to poor Lazarus who lay on the street outside his home. Lazarus died and went to the comfort of father Abraham in Heaven. The rich man died and went to a place of perpetual flames and nothing could be done to help him. Another time, Jesus watched a rich man make his offering in the Temple with considerable pomp, while a poor widow dropped only two cents in the offering. *"I tell you the truth,"* he said, *"This poor widow has put in more than all the others. She out of her poverty put in all she had to live on."* (Luke 21:3).

There is plenty of evidence to show that the people at the bottom in every society long for radical egalitarianism, in which everyone is equally eligible to be the leader. This being true, the best way to choose a leader is to cast lots, and let God decide. In Acts 1:21ff, the remaining eleven disciples decided it was important to find a replacement for Judas who betrayed Jesus. They selected two men and then cast lots, similar to dice, to decide which one of the two should take the place of Judas. Matthias was selected by lot and we never hear of him again.

A parable which emphasizes the closed mind is the story of the two sons. Jesus said a man had two sons whom he asked to work in his vineyard one day. The first son said he would not work in the vineyard but he did, while the second son said he would, but did not. Jesus' audience agreed that the first son actually did what the father wanted. Using the right words is not enough when action is required. Giving the appearance of correct belief is not enough either, when it does not lead to embracing Jesus' message about the compassionate God.

Jesus did not hesitate to challenge some ancient practices, such as the easy system of Mosaic divorce. Instead of basing his rejection on the Law of Moses, he returned to the beginning of creation in Genesis. Jesus' conclusion is in Mark's gospel, *"The two will become one flesh. So they are no longer two, but one. Therefore what God has joined together, let man not separate."* (Mark 10:8- 9). Jesus' attitude toward divorce has been a challenge for Christians ever since. We note that a Jewish man could easily divorce his wife if he no longer wanted her, but a Jewish woman could not divorce her husband. As usual, Jesus' concern was for women who had no legal standing in Jewish society apart from their husband, father or brother.

Jesus set aside the law of retaliation found in Exodus, *"If there is serious injury, you are to take life for life, eye for eye, tooth for tooth, hand for hand, foot for foot, burn for burn, wound for wound, bruise for bruise."* (Ex 21:23-25). Instead of hitting back he said, *"I tell you, do not resist an evil person. If someone strikes you on the right cheek, turn to him the other also. And if someone wants to sue you and take your tunic, let him have your cloak as well. If someone forces you to go one mile, go with him two miles."* (Matt 5:39-41 RSV). Note that a right handed person would have to use the back of his right hand to strike a person on the right cheek, which would be the blow of a superior individual against an inferior. Also note that a Palestinian man wore two garments, so that if he lost both his tunic and cloak, scholars tell us he would be naked. Admittedly, turning the other cheek and going the second mile have been difficult for many Christians. But where it has been tried, it has often worked to soften the hard and angry heart, whereas retaliation has often erupted in strife and even war. Sadly, our lower nature often prefers war.

Matthew's gospel presents Jesus as having a somewhat contradictory attitude toward the Old Testament. On the one hand

Matthew has Jesus making strong statements about the authority of the Old Testament scripture: *"Do not think that I have come to abolish the Law or the Prophets; I have not come to abolish them but to fulfill them."* (Matthew 5:17) On the other hand, Matthew has Jesus criticizing some Bible passages, re-interpreting others, often attacking traditional interpretations and even appearing to set aside the retaliation law and the taking of oaths.

In the Sermon on the Mount in Matthew's gospel we find a series of contrasts: *"You have heard it was said... but I say to you,"* followed by Jesus' deeper interpretation. With regard to murder, Jesus said: *"I say to you that everyone who is angry with his brother shall be liable to judgment; whoever insults his brother shall be liable to the council, and whoever says, 'You fool!' shall be liable to the hell of fire."* (Matt 5:22 RSV) Violence is avoided when the individual reigns in his emotions. Another example concerns the taking of an oath, or swearing to tell the truth. Jesus said, *"I tell you, do not swear at all. Let what you say be simply 'Yes' or 'No'; anything more than this comes from evil."* (Matt 5:37 RSV). Instead of saying "I swear that is what happened," he was saying simply tell the truth. Again, he referred to the Old Testament injunction to love one's neighbor and reserve hate only for enemies. But Jesus said, *"I tell you: Love your enemies and pray for those who persecute you, that you may be sons of your Father in heaven."* (Matt 5:44-45 RSV). For Christians, Jesus' interpretation is what matters.

We have only to think of those Pharisees in Jesus' audience who were working very hard day after day to please God. They were the 24/7 righteous ones who must have felt real pain to think there were those "sinners and outcasts" who might be accepted by God at the 11th hour as life's day was ending. In fact, Jesus warned his self-righteous critics that something even worse might happen: *"Jesus said to them, 'I tell you the truth, the tax collectors and the prostitutes are entering the kingdom of God ahead of you.'"* (Matt 21:31). Jesus was saying that God can accept whomever God wishes. But note again that Jesus is also saying the self-righteous ones will still get into the kingdom; they just won't be first.

71

According to one count, Jesus told 30 parables, some of which we have already referred to. Of the remainder, a few are found in only one gospel, which scholars feel reduces their historical reliability. Five are found only in Matthew's gospel: the parable of the Fishnet, the Wedding Garment, the Talents, the Ten Bridesmaids and the Weeds. A strong theme of judgment runs through each of these parables, an emphasis which is found often in Matthew's great gospel. In the parable of the Fishnet, all kinds of fish are caught when the net is pulled out of the water. The good fish are kept and the unwanted are thrown away. The parable ends, *"This is how it will be at the end of the age. The angels will come and separate the wicked from the righteous and throw them into the fiery furnace, where there will be weeping and gnashing of teeth."* (Matt 13:49-50). Note that the emphasis is not on the blessedness of the righteous, which is not even mentioned, but on the painful end of the wicked. Matthew seems to like that.

The parable of the Wedding Garment is added to the larger parable of the Wedding Banquet a king gives for his son. It is found in Matt 22:11. Luke has a similar story, not about a king, but simply about a man who gives a dinner for his friends, which we have already considered. In Matthew's version, the king enters the hall and discovers a man who is not wearing a wedding robe, even though both good and bad people had been compelled by the king's slaves to attend the banquet to make sure the wedding hall would be full. Since people were literally forced to attend, how could anyone be expected to be wearing a wedding garment? Nevertheless the king ordered his slaves to tie hand and foot the man not wearing a wedding robe, and to throw him into the outer darkness where there would be weeping and gnashing of teeth. In Luke's report on the same story, no one is punished or thrown into outer darkness.

Next in Matthew, is the parable of the Talents. Note that Luke has almost the same parable except that Luke's is the story of the pounds, not talents. Both pounds and talents are a measurement of money. In the parable, slaves are given a sum of money to invest while their owner is away. When he returns, each slave reports on how well he had invested the money, except that one slave in each parable fails to invest the money, burying or hiding it instead. In Matthew's version, the unprofitable slave is thrown *"into the outer darkness, where there will be weeping and gnashing of teeth."* (Matt 25:30 NRSV). In Luke's story, the unprofitable slave is not punished, except to lose the pound he had been given to invest. But Luke's story has an even more gruesome ending, for his slave owner is a man of noble birth, who traveled to the capitol in hopes of being made into a king. But there were some of his citizens who did not want him to be king. Unfortunately for his critics, the man of noble birth is made king and the first thing he does when he gets home is to retaliate against those who did not want him to be king: *"But those enemies of mine who did not want me to be king over them – bring them here and kill them in front of me."* (Luke 19:27). Does that sound like Jesus?

The next parable, found only in Matthew, is of the Ten Bridesmaids who are waiting for the arrival of the bridegroom. Since he is coming at night, they all have lamps. Five bridesmaids brought extra oil, but the other five did not. Their lamps are going out and the bridegroom has not arrived. While the five who did not bring extra oil are away purchasing more oil, the bridegroom arrives and the door is shut. When they return and knock on the door the bridegroom says *"Truly, I tell you, I do not know you."* (Matt 25:12 RSV). At the end of the story, Matthew adds, *"Keep awake, therefore, for you know neither the day nor the hour."* This is a clear reference to the return, or second coming of Christ, which the early Church hoped would happen at any time. The parable is a warning to be fully prepared for Jesus' return.

The fifth and final parable found only in Matthew, is the parable of the Weeds. At night, an enemy of a householder comes and plants weeds in his garden. The weeds are allowed to grow until the harvest when the wheat and weeds were bundled separately, with the wheat going into the barn while the weeds are burned. This parable comes with an interpretation which changes it into an allegory, no longer a parable. Jesus never used allegory, so this is Matthew's interpretation. He says the good seed is sown by

Jesus. The field is the world. The good seeds are the Christians and the weeds are *"the children of the evil one,"* sown by the devil. The explanation ends, *"As the weeds are pulled up and burned in the fire, so it will be at the end of the age. The Son of Man will send out his angels, and they will weed out of his kingdom everything that causes sin and all who do evil. They will throw them into the fiery furnace, where there will be weeping and gnashing of teeth."* (Matt 13:40-42). It ends with a general warning, *"Let anyone with ears, listen."* Once again, this parable, like the others found only in Matthew, is a stern warning of judgment to come. Since it is found only in Matthew, most scholars feel it is Matthew's creation. Jesus spoke of his return only in the Synoptic Apocalypse, found in Matthew 24:4-36, Mark 13:5-37 and Luke 21:8-36, writing which speculates on mostly dreadful events which will happen at the end of the world.

Both Matthew and Luke contain the short parable of the yeast or leaven, which is added at the end of the parable of the Mustard Seed. It is worded almost the same in both gospels. Jesus said, *"To what should I compare the kingdom of God? It is like yeast that a woman took and mixed in with three measures of flour until all of it was leavened."* (Luke 13:20-21 NRSV). Jesus expected his audience to discover the meaning through careful thought, which may be as follows: yeast causes the dough to expand and grow. The message of the kingdom of God, when embraced by individuals, will cause humanity to grow into its full maturity in the love and compassion of God. If this interpretation is correct, it is difficult to see how the kingdom will only be realized in some future time when God acts to establish the kingdom on earth.

The parable of the Mustard Seed is found in all three synoptic gospels. It is a parable about the growth of the kingdom. Farmers would not want the mustard plant in their gardens, since it grows so fast it can overspread the garden. It is the rapid growth of the plant which Jesus was emphasizing. It is one of the smallest seeds, yet it can grow to be a shrub so large that birds can use it for a nesting place. It is all about the rapid growth of the kingdom, which sounds like it was already beginning with Jesus' preaching and would continue on. It does not apply when the kingdom is thought of as coming at a future time when God will act to establish the kingdom on earth.

The parable of the Alert Homeowner is found in Matthew 24 and Luke 12:39ff. It is all about the second coming of the Lord. It is doubtful that Jesus ever spoke these words, since they probably reflect the longing of the Church when it ardently looked forward to Jesus' soon return. The whole parable is as follows from Matthew: *"Therefore keep watch, because you do not know on what day your Lord will come. But understand this: If the owner of the house had known at what time of night the thief was coming, he would have kept watch and would not have let his house be broken into. So you also must be ready, because the Son of Man will come at an hour when you do not expect him."* (Matt 24:42-44). We have already seen how Jesus commanded demons to be quiet when they shouted that he was the Messiah or Son of God. Again, when Peter declared Jesus to be the Messiah at Caesarea-Philippi, Jesus ordered the disciples to tell no one. So the question arises in the parable of the homeowner, why would Jesus boldly announce his second coming, even before the crucifixion and resurrection? It sounds like the belief of the church which existed when the gospels were written, fifty to sixty years after the resurrection. It is clear that Matthew is thinking of the return of Christ, for he says: *"you do not know on what day your Lord will come."* We can readily understand how the Evangelists could include beliefs of the Church when the gospels which were written many years after the time of Jesus.

The parable of the wicked tenants is found in all three Gospels. Since Mark was the first Gospel to be written, Matthew and Luke copied Mark with a few editorial changes. We are told the parable was given by Jesus during his last week in Jerusalem, just before he was crucified. In the story, a man planted a vineyard and then leased it to tenants. At the harvest the owner sent a slave to receive his share of the produce, but instead of sending the owner his share, the slave was badly beaten by the tenants. Other slaves were sent who were either beaten or killed. Finally the owner sent his beloved son in the belief they would respect him, but he also was killed. The owner then destroys the wicked tenants and hires new tenants. Jesus then quotes Psalm 118:22,23: *"The stone the builders rejected has become the capstone; the LORD has done this, and it is marvelous in our eyes."* Jesus then commented, *"Everyone who falls on that stone will be broken to pieces, but he on whom it falls will be crushed."* (Luke 20:18). When Jesus' adversaries, sent by the High Priest, heard his comment, they realized he had aimed the parable at them. They wanted to arrest him but he was too popular with the crowd.

How do we understand this parable? First, it may have come from Jesus, just as it is. He had already symbolically destroyed the Temple when he overturned the tables of the money changers. As a result, it was the High Priest's people who were monitoring Jesus' actions, so this could have been a further attack by the Lord on those who operated the Temple. However, it is doubtful that the section of the parable in reference to the owner of the vineyard sending his beloved son to collect the owner's share of the harvest actually came from Jesus. In the synoptic Gospels, Jesus refers to himself as the Son of God only once, when he was examined by the High Priest, who had already decided to have him executed. However, if the "beloved son" words are deleted, it is still a strong attack against the priests who ran the Temple. To Jesus, the priests were simply part of the domination system which caused so much pain and suffering to the majority of his people. He wanted Temple practices either reformed, with new and better leadership, or eliminated. Since his humble entrance into Jerusalem riding on a donkey clearly indicated he was not willing to use violence, he was obviously prepared to accept the consequences of his stand. The domination system he opposed now appeared ready to win another victim.

Jesus told the parable of the sower in order to show that when the good news of God's kindness and care is shared with others, some of the message will always be embraced. He intended it for his disciples and followers whom he sent out to promote his mission and message. Many farmers in Jesus' day would often broadcast their seeds over a large area, even though the ground had not been prepared to receive it. That is what the sower did in the parable with some seed falling on rocky ground, some among thorns and some on good soil. The seeds which fell on rocky and thorny ground did not grow, while seeds on good soil did take root and grow. It was a call to be faithful in sharing Jesus' good news. Not all who hear the good news will accept it, but some will.

While the above seems obvious, the explanation Jesus is reported to have given to the disciples is not. In the explanation the gospel writer has Jesus say the devil enters and prevents some from believing and so they are not saved. The truth seems to be that humans can make bad decisions without any help from the devil.

Here is the interpretation which Jesus surely intended: The "rocky ground" people receive the message with joy, but give it all up when a time of testing comes. The "thorn" people receive the message but are soon overwhelmed by cares and concerns and so lose it all. The "good soil" people are those who embrace the good news and who bear fruit quickly and abundantly. This parable may have been given by Jesus when he sent the disciples and the seventy out to the villages of Galilee to share his message of the love of God. While not all will believe and accept the message, some certainly will.

Jesus told another short parable about seeds and the growth of the kingdom of God: *"The kingdom of God is as if someone would scatter seed on the ground, and would sleep and rise, night and day, and the seed would sprout and grow, he does not know how."* (Mark 4:26-27 NRSV). Jesus was saying that just as any seed will grow without human help, following the laws of nature established by God, just so, the kingdom will grow as God directs. It appears that Jesus is saying two things about the kingdom. First, the kingdom grows through successive stages, which Jesus made clear in the comment which follows: *"...first the stalk, then the head, then the full grain in the head."* The plant, (the kingdom), does not erupt from the soil fully mature; it grows. Second, while it is God who produces the growth of the kingdom, it still requires someone

– a faithful follower of Jesus – who is needed to scatter the seed. Finally, the kingdom grows; it is not reserved for God alone to establish the kingdom in its fullness at the end of time. God has decided to use the devoted efforts of his faithful children to broadcast the message, by sharing the good news. God will take care of the growth by working in the hearts and thinking of people, helping them to respond.

Luke has the parable of the widow and the unjust judge. The widow is unable to get the judge to decide her case against a man who has wronged her. The judge does not want to be bothered with her complaint, but that does not stop the widow who keeps insisting on justice. Finally the judge takes up her case and decides in her favor to keep her from wearing him out. Jesus says God is better than the judge and will answer the prayers of his children when they cry to him for justice. Luke correctly introduces the parable by saying: *"Jesus told them a parable about their need to pray always and not to lose heart."* (Luke 18:1 NRSV). God answers prayer. It has been pointed out many times that God's answer may be "no," "maybe" or "later," which requires a high degree of Christian patience and trust.

At this point, let us look at something which is not a parable, but a strange incident reported in all three synoptics, the healing of the Gadarene (or Gerasene) demoniac. Some scholars are sure this never really happened since it has every appearance of being a verbal attack against the Roman occupation. Perhaps it may have arisen just before the rebellion of the Jews against Rome in 67-70 CE, in which they were horribly crushed.

We are told that Jesus and the disciples crossed over the Sea of Galilee and entered the gentile area of the Gerasenes (Gadarenes in Matthew's version). He is immediately confronted by a man possessed by demons. The demoniac tells Jesus he is inhabited by a whole legion of demons. Legion is the word for a large unit of Roman soldiers. Jesus casts the legion of demons out of the man, allowing them to go into a herd of pigs feeding nearby. The pigs rush down the hill and plunge into the sea and are drowned. We note that neither the towns of Gadara or Gerasa are on the Sea of

Galilee, which makes it impossible for the herd to plunge into the sea, if they were near either of those towns. The people who owned the pigs ask Jesus to leave and he departs. They are not Jews who would have nothing to do with pigs.

The reason some scholars doubt the authenticity of this story is that it fits so neatly into a story designed to encourage Jews to laugh at the plight of the Romans who are easily identified as the legion of demons inside the man. Look at what happens to the legion of "Roman" demons: they are sent headlong into the waters, which is exactly what most Jews would want them to do; get into their boats and sail back to Rome. But there is more. The Roman demons are sent into pigs, the most distasteful but also the most desirable destination for Roman legions in the thinking of Jewish patriots. And then the pigs, now inhabited by the legion of Romans, rush into the water and are drowned. Was this an event which really happened in the ministry of Jesus, or was it a story which circulated at or near the time when the Jews rebelled against the Roman occupation in 66–70 CE? We can be reasonably sure Jesus would also want the Roman Legions to go back to Rome where they belonged.

This Is My Beloved Son

Chapter 9

THE CHALLENGE OF THE BIBLE

The Bible is indispensable for Christian living. It is vital for faith because it begins with God, continues with God and ends with God like no other book. The main character is God. Scripture can be seen as a record of God reaching out to people and people responding to God as they were able, within the confines of their own personal and social limitations. It begins with an ancient understanding of God, and ends with the seeking and saving love of the God Jesus knew and proclaimed. Many passages in the Bible, like the 23rd Psalm, the 53rd chapter of Isaiah, the Sermon on the Mount, the 13th chapter of first Corinthians, and dozens of others, and hundreds of single verses, lead to the conviction that God is involved in the things which deeply concern humans. Through God's acts recorded in Scripture, and above all through Jesus, we can know what God is like and even come to know, love and trust the living God.

The Bible is an ancient book, but it is also part of an unfinished story. The lives of the people of the Bible are different from our own, but their experience of God and the issues of life which they faced are surprisingly similar to ours. We are united with them across the centuries in the continuing drama of finding our way to meaning, hope and God. From the story of creation, the lives of the patriarchs, (Abraham, Isaac and Jacob), the rise and fall of the nation Israel, the teaching, death and resurrection of Jesus, the coming of the Holy Spirit on Pentecost, to the beginning of the Christian Church, the Bible witnesses to the action of God reaching out in amazing grace to men and women, boys and girls, young and old. In each generation and indeed in every human life, the Spirit of God calls people through Scripture and prayerful meditation to respond to the divine love in wholehearted commitment. The Bible finds its center and unifying truth in Jesus. To many, he appeared out of nowhere with an amazing authority which challenged and consoled, while pointing always to the totally trustworthy God whose love never fails. As God came to the ancient ones, so the God who was in Jesus comes to us, challenging us to join the long caravan of faithful pilgrims who know there is more to life than we can see or touch.

Christians have always regarded the Bible as a special revelation from God. Multitudes have eagerly read its pages, looking for some story or verse which would help them meet a special need in their lives. And they have found it. Those facing grief over the loss of a loved one have turned to Paul's letter to the Romans: *"I am convinced that neither death nor life, neither the present nor the future, neither height nor depth, nor anything else in all creation, will be able to separate us from the love of God that is in Christ Jesus our Lord."* (Romans 8:38-39).

Others, troubled by some personal issue, will find encouragement in the prayer of the Psalmist, *"Turn to me and be gracious to me, for I am lonely and afflicted. Relieve the troubles of my heart, and bring me out of my distress."* (Psalm 25:16f NRSV). The lonely individual who needs some joy might find needed direction and encouragement in Paul's letter to the Christians in the city of Philippi, *"Rejoice in the Lord always. I will say it again: Rejoice! The Lord is near. Do not be anxious about anything, but in everything, by prayer and petition, with thanksgiving, present your requests to God. And the peace of God, which transcends all understanding, will guard your hearts and your minds in Christ Jesus."* (Phil 4:4-7). Or we might embrace this passage from John's Gospel, *"As the Father has loved me, so have I loved you. Now remain in my love. I have told you this so that my joy may be in you and that your joy may be complete."* (John 15:9-11). On page after page, helpful verses are found.

But while the Bible is looked upon as the revelation of God, there has never been a unanimous explanation as to how this is true. Neither is there full agreement as to how the Bible is to be applied when it is regarded as God's revelation. Scripture itself is often used to prove the absolute authority of the Bible: *"All Scripture is inspired by God and is useful for teaching, for reproof, for correction, and for training in righteousness."* (2nd Timothy 3:16 NRSV).This is one of the last books of the New Testament to be written and the author was no doubt referring to the Old Testament when he speaks of "all Scripture." But this can hardly be accepted as a description of the Bible's inspiration since the phrase, "all Scripture is inspired by God," is not explained. It could not have referred to the New Testament since most of the New Testament was not yet regarded as sacred Scripture. In addition, this verse only says that Scripture is "profitable for teaching, for reproof, for correction and for training in righteousness;" it does not say it is perfectly inspired or that God dictated, word for word, exactly what God wanted.

The writers of the various books were not without their own minds, clearly seen in the differences in style of writing, the vocabulary used and the quality of writing. The inspiration is not in the Scripture; the inspiration comes to the individual from the Holy Spirit who leads us to God's truth through the "still, small voice." According to John's gospel Jesus said, *"When he, the Spirit of truth comes, he will guide you into all truth."* (John 16:13). The Spirit of truth is the Holy Spirit, the third Person of the Trinity, whom the Apostle Paul taught resides in every believing and trusting soul.

For years in the early Christian Church, the only recognized scripture was the Old Testament. Only 11 books of the Old Testament are not referred to in the New Testament. But when they quoted it, the quotations were sometimes inaccurate and sometimes a blending of quotes from two different Old Testament sources. In addition, Christians set aside much of the Old Testament as no longer relevant. The whole sacrificial system involving animal sacrifices was set aside by the early Christians in favor of a personal relationship with the living Christ and the inner direction of the Holy Spirit.

Often missed, when reading the Old Testament, is the fact of development from older to later beliefs and practices. There is major development in the perception of God from the God of the Exodus and the giving of the Law under Moses, to the ethical God of the prophets. At least five times the Book of Deuteronomy says God's wrath was "provoked" as the Israelites wandered through the Exodus wilderness. Time after time, God destroyed large numbers of the people when they dared to complain about the hardships they endured. The fickleness of the people was matched by the wrathfulness of God.

It is good for us to admit there is much we do not know or understand, not only in religion, but with regard to the huge mass of knowledge available to the individual today. Discoveries are being made and confirmed, especially in subatomic particles, which seem to contradict reason. Scientists tell us there is a lot of dark matter in space, but they don't know where it is. We respond with pity and humor to the story attributed to Pope Gregory the Great who told of a nun who ate lettuce without making the sign of the cross and thereby swallowed a devil. Today, because of scientific and medical advances, people who claim to believe in devils and demons might humorously be accused of being possessed. However, missionaries to remote places still occasionally report cases regarded by the local people as demon possession.

However, knowing a lot about the Bible is not required for hearing the voice of the Spirit speaking through Scripture. However, ignorance is no help either. Most of the hard work in understanding the Bible has been done for us by dedicated Christian scholars who have spent a lifetime in its study. Prayer, from the heart, which seeks the inner direction of God's Spirit, is most important. But prayer alone may result in the Spirit loudly thundering "study and learn." We remember that Jesus wanted a balance between learning and action. He said, *"Take my yoke upon you and learn from me."* He also said, *"Why do you call me, 'Lord, Lord,' but do not do what I tell you?"* (Luke 6:46,47). The Bible student is the one *"who hears my* (Jesus') *words and puts them into practice."* (Luke 6:47). Doing the words of Jesus is as important as knowing them, and that comes through persistent study and prayer for the inner direction of the Holy Spirit enabling us to put what we have learned into practice.

The compassionate God of Jesus is not found in all parts of the Bible. The Biblical literalists are wrong when they claim there is no contradiction between believing in the God of Jesus and the God of Moses at Mt Sinai. If true, then why did the terrified people say to Moses: *"Speak to us yourself and we will listen. But do not have God speak to us or we will die."* (Ex 20:19). Jesus, on the other hand, strongly urged people, not only to trust the unfailing love of God, but to imitate God in daily experience and in all relationships. The imitation of the God Jesus spoke of leads to life and not death.

Speaking of Moses, there is that strange episode recorded in Ex 4:24 when God tried to kill Moses because he apparently neglected to circumcise his infant son.

Then there is the ruthless God of the prophet Samuel who, believing he was speaking with God's authority, told King Saul that he must surprise attack the Amalekites and kill every man, woman and child. (See I Samuel 15:2,3). According to Samuel, King Saul was to do this because many years before, the Amalekites had resisted the Children of Israel when they escaped from Egypt and came too close to their territory when the Israelites were on their way to the Promised Land. King Saul obediently killed everyone, but for some strange reason, took captive the king of the Amalakites instead of killing him, whereupon Samuel in a rage took a sword and cut the king of the Amalekites in pieces. Was Samuel correct? Did God demand the Amalekites be destroyed for something their great grandparents had done? If so, what kind of God are we dealing with? Can we worship this God or should we hide?

The Bible has many contrary teachings such as, *"Vengeance is mine, and recompense, for the time when their foot shall slip; for the day of their calamity is at hand, and their doom comes swiftly."* (Deut 32:35 RSV). The Apostle Paul quotes this passage in

Romans: *"Beloved, never avenge yourselves, but leave it to the wrath of God; for it is written, 'Vengeance is mine, I will repay, says the Lord.' No, if your enemy is hungry, feed him; if he is thirsty, give him drink."* (Romans 12:19-20 RSV). But note that Jesus does not leave it to the wrath of God; he sets the intent of Deuteronomy aside when he insists that the way to handle an enemy is with love, *"You have heard that it was said, 'Love your neighbor and hate your enemy.' But I tell you: Love your enemies and pray for those who persecute you, that you may be sons of your Father in heaven."* (Matt 5:43-45 RSV). It is obvious there is a distinct difference between the God of Samuel and the God of Jesus.

What are we to think when all the Israelites stoned to death, not an enemy, but one of their own, a man who had sinned by gathering some sticks for firewood on the Sabbath? (Numbers 15:35f).

Then there is Achan and his wife and children, his animals and all his material possessions. His family and animals were stoned to death and burned along with all his possessions by all the Israelites because he had taken a garment, some silver and a bar of gold when Jericho was destroyed. The order was that everything in Jericho was to be destroyed. But Achan took these things and paid a heavy price for his disobedience. There is little or no mercy or forgiveness in the earlier parts of the Old Testament Bible. What happened to Achan and his family is the direct outcome of Ex 20:5 where God is presented as saying, *"I, the LORD your God, am a jealous God, punishing the children for the sin of the fathers to the third and fourth generation of those who hate me, but showing love to a thousand generations of those who love me and keep my commandments."* (Ex 20:5-6). Are we to believe that God will not only punish a man who sins, but also punish his grandchildren, great grandchildren, even to the fourth generation, just because Exodus 20:5 says God is a jealous God who takes delight in punishing the innocent children of a sinful parent? Exodus 20 does go on to say God gives his love to thousands of generations of those who love him. In other words, our love for God causes or releases God's love for us, which is contrary to the clear teaching of Jesus that God's love is given and does not need to be earned by our love, or by anything else we may feel required to do. This is a supreme example of development in the understanding of God, and it comes from Jesus.

There are laws in the Bible which require the death of anyone who engages in adultery or in murder. But apparently if you were important enough, you could get away with both. King David, whom Scripture says was "a man after God's own heart," committed both crimes. He engaged in adultery with Bathsheba and then had her husband killed who was fighting for the king, in the king's army. Any other man in David's kingdom would have been executed, but God decided not to kill David. Instead, God decided to kill the child which David fathered with Bathsheba. Is that justice? The Prophet Nathan revealed to the king that God knew all about the terrible thing he had done in committing adultery and then having Uriah the Hittite, the husband of Bathsheba, killed in battle. But Nathan, speaking for God, said: *"You shall not die. Nevertheless, because by this deed you have utterly scorned the LORD, the child that is born to you shall die."* (2 Sam 12:13-14 NRSV). David should have died, but because he is the king, his unborn child will die instead. It was Jesus who took little children in his arms and blessed them.

A far different understanding of human fatherhood and the fatherhood of God is given by Jesus who taught that God's love for his children is much greater than the love of human parents. All people are the children of God who is the supreme parent, whose love does not have to be earned and which never fails, who forgives even though the sinner does not ask forgiveness. Which God should we choose: The God of Jesus or the God of Nathan?

There is a redemptive side to David which has to do with the prophecy of Nathan, who told David that his son, born of the adulterous union with Bathsheba, would die instead of David. True to the prophet's prophecy, the little boy baby got seriously ill. For days, David prayed to God for the boy; he lay on the ground and refused any food. After seven days, the baby died and David's advisors were afraid to tell David, not knowing what he might do. David suspected that the child was dead and, to everyone's surprise, he took a bath, anointed himself and entered the Temple to worship God. Only then did he eat any food. He said he fasted and prayed, holding on to the hope that God might let the child live. But since the boy had died, there was no point in continuing to fast and pray. He said, *"I will go to him, but he cannot come to me."*

Nevertheless, the dark side of David cannot be hidden. Consider King David's concern for the Gibeonites who were said to have suffered at the direction of King Saul, who preceded David as king. We are told David felt deep regret for the Gibeonite survivors of Saul's action, even though the Gibeonites were not Israelites. David asked them what could be done to make right what had happened to them years before, allegedly at the direction of King Saul. The result was that seven of King Saul's sons were turned over to the Gibeonites who hung them on a mountain tree and left them there to decompose. It is obvious that King David had found a way to eliminate some of the sons of King Saul who might be a threat to his hold on the kingship. We are told that this action concerning the Gibeonites pleased God who promptly ended a three year old famine. How could God be pleased with David's transparent, self-serving action? And is the Bible wrong about the famine?

David was highly successful in war, extending his kingdom in all directions. He defeated the Moabites and to make sure they could not retaliate, he killed two out of three of their captured soldiers. David apparently did not remember that his great-grandmother, Ruth, was a Moabite who had married the Israelite, Boaz. They had a son and "they named him Obed. He was the father of Jesse, the father of David." (Ruth 4:17 NRSV).

In much of the Old Testament there is no hope for life after death. At some point in time belief in Sheol developed as a place where the dead go, a place of darkness and silence, with nothing that resembles the prior life. The Old Testament book of Ecclesiastes says of Sheol, *"Whatever your hand finds to do, do with your might; for there is no work or thought or knowledge or wisdom in Sheol, to which you are going."* (Eccl 9:10 NRSV).

Sometime after the return of the Jews from their captivity in Babylon, belief in life after this life began to emerge. But not everyone believed it. In the time of Jesus, the wealthy Sadducees, who put their security in their money, were certain that this life is all there is. How much more helpful is the Christian hope of life eternal based on faith in the goodness of God. Death is not a door which shuts and no one can open it; it is a door which opens into God's eternity. In Paul's first letter to the Christians in Corinth, he says: *"Death has been swallowed up in victory. Where, O death, is your victory? Where, O death, is your sting?"* (1 Cor 15:54-55 NRSV). John's Gospel has this reassuring promise from Jesus, *"Because I live, you also will live."* (John 14:19 NRSV). Without knowing all the answers, Christians proclaim life eternal with conviction and joy and trust in God.

Many early Christian leaders challenged much that is presented in the Bible. Origin felt it was foolish to believe, as Genesis records, that there could be a first, second and third day before the sun, moon and stars were created, and that all you had to do to gain wisdom was for Adam and Eve to take one bite of the fruit of the tree of the knowledge of good and evil in the garden. It shocked Origin that God should be pictured as a man so frequently. He felt it was blasphemous to take such things literally. He even said the New Testament gospels should not be taken literally either, because, he said, there were "discrepancies, contradictions and impossibilities" in them. The Jewish scholar, Philo of Alexandria wrote: "It is a sign of great simplicity to think the world could be created in six days, that a woman was made out of a man's rib, that Cain actually built a city all by himself; such things are contrary to all reason." However, Origin solved the challenge of difficult passages in Scripture through the use of allegory, as we shall see a little later.

Today, how many believe the sun stood still as recorded in Joshua 10:12, or that Elisha's bones brought a dead man back to life or that on the day of the resurrection of Jesus, dead people came up out of their graves and walked around Jerusalem, as recorded in Matthew 27:52f. And how are we to understand the strange story in Gen 6:2-4, where some kind of heavenly beings, called the Sons of God, married earthly women? In the past, this was interpreted to have happened because some angels rebelled, were evicted from heaven, and as a result married human women and produced demon children. If you are ever tempted to call your child a "little devil," you can be sure it is not evidence that there is truth in the Genesis story about fallen angels. Also, we need to remember whose child it is when we call him or her a little devil.

The general rule was that the interpretation of Scripture must be in keeping with the Christian faith as it is accepted "everywhere, always and by everyone." In the Middle Ages, the tendency was to confine interpretation of the Bible to the conclusions reached by the early Church Fathers. These were bishops or leaders in the large cities of the Roman Empire in the first five centuries of the Christian era. In the time of the reformation, Martin Luther rejected the rule that interpretation of Scripture belonged to the Pope alone. He felt that every competent Christian was capable of understanding and embracing the Bible's message. Luther and all reformers taught that the Holy Spirit was the final authority and that Scripture's center is in Jesus Christ. Those parts of the Bible which are in keeping with Jesus are most authoritative.

Three ways were used to interpret the Bible: Literally, Morally or Allegorically. The Literal had its weakness, for the Scripture spoke of the arm of God, the eyes of God and God's backside, which, if taken literally, meant that God is a very big man. The moral application was dependent on the literal meaning, but was often ignored in favor of the allegorical interpretation. Allegory opened the door to a flood of possibilities. Any time a passage was difficult to explain, it was assumed there must be a hidden meaning in it and the hidden meaning could be almost anything the Bible teacher or preacher decided, using allegory. Even today, many literal minded Christians find they cannot accept the Old Testament book, Song of Songs, for what it truly is: a celebration of sexual love between a man and a woman. So instead, it is interpreted allegorically as the love of Christ for His Bride, the Church, or given some other interpretation which misses the truth entirely. By the way, the word church is nowhere mentioned in the Song. In some Bibles, the Song of Songs is called the Song of Solomon, perhaps because it was felt King Solomon ought to know all about sexual love since he had three hundred wives and seven hundred concubines.

For Origen, the solution to the difficulties he found in the Bible was through the use of allegory. Anything that was too difficult to accept was simply reinterpreted in a more acceptable way. So on the first Palm Sunday, when the Gospel of Matthew mistakenly says Jesus entered Jerusalem riding on two animals, Origen said that one animal was the Old Testament and the other the New Testament. What difference that made is difficult to imagine, but it probably made for interesting preaching, though not recommended for most of today's congregations. Both Origen and Matthew failed to explain how Jesus could ride into Jerusalem on two animals, a feat which is found only in Matthew's Gospel. Through allegory, the Scripture could be forced to deliver any meaning the preacher determined. The Bible scholar, Wycliffe, interpreted Jesus' parable of the Good Samaritan as an allegory. He said the victim in the parable represented the first parents, Adam and Eve, the robbers were the devils from Hell, the Priest and Levite were the Patriarchs and the Prophets who failed to bring salvation to the needy and the good Samaritan was Jesus. That is allegory at work.

For John Calvin, father of the Reformed (Presbyterian) family of churches, "the author of Scripture is God." Calvin, Luther and other reformers broke the hold of allegory. Calvin said "We must entirely reject the allegories of Origen and of others like him." Jesus faced the same challenge in Bible interpretation, but he never resorted to allegory, although he is reported to have interpreted one of his own parables allegorically. There is almost no allegory in the New Testament. Calvin, and other Protestant Reformers, taught that "the true meaning of Scripture is the natural and obvious meaning." He left no room for allegory.

Calvin came close to affirming the inerrancy of the Bible, but he admitted there were minor errors in it. While he wrote commentaries on most books of the Bible, he did not do so for the Song of Songs or the Revelation. He said he was completely unable to discover the meaning of the Revelation. Calvin affirmed that there is progressive revelation in the Bible from the OT to the NT. However, deadly literalism took the place of allegory in Protestant churches. Many have been brought up on Calvin's literalism. For him, the serpent literally talked to Eve in the Garden of Eden as recorded in the book of Genesis; God literally made the first woman out of one of Adam's ribs; Noah's ark was literally filled with samples of all living creatures so they would not drown, like nearly all humans did; the strength of Samson was literally in his hair, which he lost when Delilah cut his hair as he slept; the details of the tabernacle were literally revealed to Moses on Mt Sinai; God literally wrote the 10 commandments on stone with his finger. For some reason, God literally revealed his backside to Moses on Mount Sinai and God literally commanded the massacre of all the Canaanites so the invading Israelites could take their villages, homes, fields and orchards.

In the period following the Reformation, interest in the Bible was very high, but also stifled by dogmatism in which both Protestants and Roman Catholics declared they had the correct and only way to understand the Bible. For Catholics, every interpretation must be in keeping with that given by the hierarchy of the church. But more people were thinking their own thoughts. In time there was the development of biblical criticism, which simply meant the careful and unfettered examination of the Bible by scholars who were not afraid to ask questions. Critical study simply gave to Scripture the same careful and precise examination which was used in the study of any ancient writing and which science was now following in the exploration of the material world. This careful study eventually liberated the human mind from the narrow confines of verbal inspiration and inerrancy. The result was that the Bible was studied more carefully than ever before as scholars looked into the authorship, date, composition and meaning of every book of the Bible. The result was a deepening appreciation for the wonder of Scripture which contains a helpful and progressive message about God and humanity, culminating in the life and ministry of Jesus.

This careful study of Holy Scripture led many Christians to understand that the Bible must not be given an authority which is higher than the authority of Jesus or higher than the authority of the living God. The Bible must be evaluated in much the same way as we view our Lord Jesus Christ. Christians long ago determined that Jesus was both fully human and fully divine. To appreciate Christ's impact on the life of mankind, both the humanity and deity of Jesus must be considered. The same is even truer of the Bible. It is a sad mistake to disregard Scripture's humanity. In the Gospel of John, Jesus said to his disciples that the Holy Spirit would lead them into all truth. He did not say the Scripture would lead them into all truth, partly because little of the New Testament was yet written. God did not come to us in Jesus Christ and then depart after the resurrection, leaving only a book behind. The main emphasis in both the Old and New Testaments is that God not only acts in history, but God is still the main actor in today's history as the Holy Spirit leads people to accept the new life which is available through faithfully following Jesus Christ and adopting his way.

Literalism prevented the church from new discoveries, especially with regard to the sun, moon and stars. There was little astronomy in the church since the serious study of the stars was discouraged. Many people appeared to believe in Astrology, that the stars influence and even control human events. The Copernican system, which declared that the earth goes around the sun and not the sun around the earth, caused a violent reaction among church leaders. The Catholic Church condemned it and Martin Luther said Copernicus was a fool for suggesting that the earth moved around the sun. They believed the first chapters of Genesis gave the correct account of creation. While few educated people accept that today, we recognize that the Genesis story of creation was a giant step forward when it first appeared in ancient times. The non-

Biblical Babylonian religious parallels are full of the antics of the Gods, including fear of dragons, with spirits in everything. Instead of polytheism the Bible presents us with ethical monotheism. And in place of mythology, we have a personal and transcendent God.

There must be a great many people who get interested in the Bible, discover they cannot accept parts of it and cannot understand even more, and so give up and turn aside to other interests. What we actually have among conservative Christians is people believing almost anything which they solidly base on some part of the Bible, ignoring other parts which do not agree with their conclusions. The truth is the Bible must be and always is interpreted by whoever reads it. Two people reading the same passage may get two very different interpretations of its meaning and importance. It is almost always true that we interpret the Bible in keeping with the values we had adopted before we opened the Scripture. If we believe in capital punishment, we will find many passages which support that belief. But the person who is opposed to capital punishment is almost certain to point to Jesus' refusal to throw a stone at the woman caught in the act of adultery, as the Old Testament Law obligated him to do, (John 8:1-11). In American history, slavery was promoted by church people on Biblical grounds.

Knowing the facts in Scripture does not bring us to God or make us better Christians. Literalism does not make a person a better Christian either. To be a Bible Christian, is to be open to the direction of the Holy Spirit and to have a vital relationship with the God of Jesus, the kind of relationship he had with God and urged others to adopt.

When we see Jesus as God's supreme effort to bring truth and hope to humanity, then we know how indispensable is Scripture, especially the Gospels which give us our only record of the ministry of the Lord. However, the Gospels were not written by eye-witnesses, giving us factual and objective reports of the things Jesus said and did. The Gospels are interpreted remembrances, written long after the events described in them. They were designed to promote the faith which believers were following at the time when the Gospels were written.

In his annual Easter letter to the churches in 367CE, Athanasius, the bishop of Alexandria, Egypt gave a list of the books to be included in the New Testament. It contained all 27 books found in our New Testament today. So we can say the official content or canon of the New Testament was fixed by that date. Both the Revelation and the book of Hebrews had the greatest difficulty getting included. The Revelation has always been difficult to understand and apply. The book of Hebrews may have emphasized good works instead of faith alone.

How should we read the Bible? To understand and appreciate the Bible some presuppositions need to be set aside. It is not a book of science. It is much more important than that, for science only deals with what and how something happened, while the Bible seeks to explain why it happened and our response to it. Science can tell us a great deal about how the earth was created and how humans arrived, while the Bible seeks to explain why we are here and how best to live our lives. The Bible is not a book of science, neither is it to be viewed as great literature. The purpose of its writers was not to produce beautiful verse, but to point people to the real possibility of a wonderful relationship with others and with the living God. Ultimately it is the God revealed so beautifully in Jesus.

Many churches believe that without the inspiration of the Holy Spirit, there is no "saving knowledge of Scripture." The ultimate authority for Christians is God the Holy Spirit, not the Bible. It would appear that those who hold up the Bible as their ultimate authority are unknowingly committing the ancient sin of idolatry by allowing a material thing to be worshipped in place of the living God. The inspiration of Holy Scripture is not in the book, but in the person who studies the Scripture and whose mind is open to receive the guidance of the Spirit, and whose conclusions are modified when compared with the conclusions of others.

The learning Jesus called for includes much that is in the Old Testament, which has a lot to offer especially when we get into the later writings. The book of Job is an example. It was written during or after the exile, as a protest against the belief that those who suffer illness or poverty are being punished by God. We noted earlier that Satan was a member of the heavenly court as one of God's counselors, whose responsibility was to challenge and test the faith of God's people. It was during the Babylonian captivity, however, that Satan became wicked and worked to defeat the purposes of God. He was believed to exist in fire where the guilty go for punishment. He could enter a person's heart and take control, as he did with Judas. Satan has many demons and devils able to seize control of individuals and cause great suffering. Satan was the explanation for evil in human experience. Jesus' victory over evil and Satan is a major theme in the gospels.

In the book of Job, God gave Satan the right to test Job in whatever way Satan desired, which raises questions about God, but this is fiction. Satan begins by stripping Job of all his wealth. Then all Job's children are killed in an unusual accident. Finally, Job himself is afflicted with excruciating sores like boils all over his body. Three of Job's friends come to encourage him. When they saw him, his appearance was so changed by his sufferings, they lifted up their voices and wept aloud, tore their robes and sprinkled dust on their heads. They sat with Job for seven days and seven nights before they said anything. Our presence is sometimes the best comfort we can give to someone who is grieving. When they did speak, they tried to help Job by convincing him that he must have sinned terribly which is why God is angry at him, and if he would only confess his faults, God might show mercy and his pain would end. This is the theme of the book: why do the innocent suffer?

Throughout the book, Job insists he has never done anything to cause God to turn against him the way he has. His anger at God is complete. He finally declares his belief that there must be an advocate or intercessor, someone who will condemn what God has done and vindicate Job. Some Bible versions wrongly interpret the word advocate as "redeemer," which they declare has been fulfilled in Jesus. A song has been written which says "I know that my redeemer lives," based on this verse in Job. But Job longs for an advocate who can judge between him and God, and he is sure this advocate will decide in Job's favor. The book of Job ends when God appears to Job and subdues him with many words like these: *"Where were you when I laid the foundations of the earth? Tell me, if you understand."* (Job 38:4 RSV). Job has no good answer. He is overwhelmed by God, although the Lord never deals directly with Job's questions. Job says, *"I had heard of thee by the hearing of the ear, but now my eye sees thee; therefore I despise myself, and repent in dust and ashes."* (Job 42:5-6 RSV). In the end, the sufferer can only trust God. While Job is angry with God throughout the book, he never gives up his belief that there was an answer.

Another book which merits our attention is the book of Proverbs which extols the virtues of wisdom. The Greek word for wisdom is Sophia. Proverbs presents wisdom (Sophia) as present with God at the moment of creation, *"By wisdom the LORD laid the earth's foundations,"* (Prov 3:19). These verses identify wisdom as feminine: *"Do not forsake wisdom, and she will protect you; love her, and she will watch over you. Wisdom is supreme; therefore get wisdom. Though it cost all you have, get understanding. Esteem her, and she will exalt you; embrace her, and she will honor you. She will set a garland of grace on your head and present you with a crown of splendor."* (Prov 4:6-9). By contrast, the first chapter of John's gospel, says the "Word" was present with God when the world was created: *"In the beginning was the Word, and the Word was with God, and the Word was God. He was with God in the beginning. Through him all things were made; without him nothing was made that has been made."* (John 1:1-3). When John used the word "Word," we are sure he was referring to Jesus. In recent years some women have experimented with finding a way to make use of Sophia from Proverbs to add a little gender balance, especially since the very next verse in John is thoroughly masculine: *"In him was life, and that life was the light of men."* (John 1:4 RSV).

What can be said about Ecclesiastes, another Old Testament book? About the only part of this book which is ever used in worship is from chapter three which says, *"There is a time for everything, and a season for every activity under heaven: a time to be born and a time to die, a time to plant and a time to uproot, a time to kill and a time to heal, a time to tear down and a time to build, a time to weep and a time to laugh, a time to mourn and a time to dance."* (Eccl 3:1-4). The theme of the book is set forth in the opening verses, spoken by the "Teacher:" *" 'Meaningless! Meaningless!' says the Teacher. 'Utterly meaningless, everything is meaningless. What does man gain from all his labor at which he toils under the sun?' "* (Eccl 1:2-3). God is mentioned in Ecclesiastes, but usually in a guarded sense: *"When times are good, be happy; but when times are bad, consider: God has made the one as well as the other. Therefore, a man cannot discover anything about his future."* (Eccl 7:14). Much of what is found in this great book is true to those times in life when God is felt to be distant and unknowable. The hard knocks of life are easier to accept when life is lived trusting the God revealed in Jesus.

We have already mentioned the book of Psalms, often referred to as the hymnbook of the Bible. In fact, some Protestant churches sing psalms only and no other hymns. The psalms run the full range of human experience, all the way from fear to confidence, from love to hate, from friends to enemies. It is surprising how often enemies and foes are referred to. One gets the impression that next door neighbors must keep an eye on each other. The Psalmist sometimes complains about the lack of God's care: *"Why, O LORD, do you stand far off? Why do you hide yourself in times of trouble?"* (Psalm 10:1 NRSV). Also this verse: *"Answer me when I call to you, O my righteous God. Give me relief from my distress; be merciful to me and hear my prayer."* (Psalm 4:1). There are dozens of psalms worthy of memorization: *"You show me the path of life. In your presence there is fullness of joy; in your right hand are pleasures forevermore."* (Psalm 16:11 NRSV).

Some Psalms speak of the wonder of creation, such as Psalm 8, already mentioned, and Psalm 19 in which the vast universe talks: *"The heavens declare the glory of God; the skies proclaim the work of his hands. Day after day they pour forth speech; night after night they display knowledge. There is no speech or language where their voice is not heard."* (Psalms 19:1-3). There is also that sad Psalm 22, which speaks of the sorrow of intense suffering. Jesus quoted the first verse as he hung on the cross: *"My God, my God, why have you forsaken me?"* (Psalm 22:1 NRSV). The very next psalm, 23, is the best known in the Psalter. Other psalms offer hope in difficult times: *"This poor man cried, and the LORD heard him, and saved him out of all his troubles."* (Psalm 34:6 RSV). In a time when there was no medical care, illness could be terrifying: *"I am bowed down and brought very low; all day long I go about mourning. My back is filled with searing pain; there is no health in my body."* (Psalm 38:6-7). There is praise when health returns: *"I waited patiently for the LORD; he inclined to me and heard my cry. He put a new song in my mouth, a song of praise to our God."* (Psalm 40:1,3 NRSV). It is a helpful practice to highlight or mark those verses which have personal value, and there are many, not only in the Psalms but throughout the Bible.

The O. T. books of Ezra and Nehemiah cover the time in Jewish history when the Persian King, Cyrus the Great, permitted the Jews to return to Jerusalem after their exile in Babylon. Many did return while large numbers preferred remaining in Babylon. One of the first decisions by the returnees was not to allow the people who were already living in and around Jerusalem to assist them in rebuilding the walls and the temple. Most of those already living in the area were Jews who had not been deported when the Babylonian King Nebuchadnezzar defeated the kingdom of Judah in 586 BCE. Ezra and Nehemiah utterly refused to have anything to do with these people who had often intermarried with other inhabitants. More than once, they forced Jews who had come with them from Babylon to marry only Jewish women, and in cases where marriages had already taken place, they forced Jewish men to abandon their wives and children. One of the men spoke to Ezra, saying, *"We have been unfaithful to our God by marrying foreign women from the peoples around us. But in spite of this, there is still hope for Israel. Now let us make a covenant before our God to send away all these women and their children."* (Ezra 10:2-3). We cannot help but wonder what happened to those women, and the children who no longer had a father. Under Ezra and Nehemiah, it was necessary for everyone to prove the purity of their Jewish lineage.

Then there is the Book of Esther, a book of pure fiction, in which neither the word God nor prayer appear. However, it forms the basis for the Jewish feast of Purim. It is a story of the deliverance of the Jewish people in the time of the Persian Empire. Through the efforts of the official, Haman, the Jews were to be freely slaughtered on a given day throughout the empire and their possessions taken by their enemies. However, the plot was miraculously thwarted and reversed, with Jews throughout the empire legally empowered to slaughter their enemies instead. While it provides little spiritual encouragement, it does show the need for hope to people who have endured long persecution.

By the time of the Prophets, the God of the Exodus wilderness has become the source and example of justice and compassion. It is no longer fear of God, but the imitation of God which the prophets said was important. They talked more about the justice of God and not as much about God's righteousness, wrath and holiness. With the prophets it is truly possible to love the Lord your God "with all your heart, mind and strength." The highest development is in the life and message of Jesus who never pointed to a deity who prowls the hills and valleys looking for evildoers to devour, but to the God of compassion who never fails to love his children.

Ever since the Protestant Reformation, the Bible has been the most read and studied document ever produced. It may also be the least understood book, and in recent times it has too often been the seldom read book on the believers' shelves. That may be because educated Christians find the Bible to have a surprising number of contradictions, while asking the reader to believe things which were accepted in an ancient time, but which are unacceptable in today's world. And, of course, there is television and sports which many may feel is much more important. Perhaps those who take the Bible seriously, including people who believe in the literal interpretation or Biblical inerrancy, still have trouble believing in demon possession, or the Genesis account of how the world began or apocalyptic ideas about the end of the world or the eternal punishment of sinners in Hell.

Thinking believers are bound to ask how Jesus was able to heal the sick and cast out evil spirits. The answer is we simply do not know. But it is clear that Jesus was able to heal and help many. We recognize that there were others in Jesus' day also recognized as healers and exorcists. When he was accused by his critics of casting out demons by Satan's power, he said, *"If I cast out demons by Be-el'zebul (Satan), by whom do your sons cast them out? Therefore they shall be your judges."* (Matt 12:27 RSV). Mark has a record of another exorcist operating nearby: *"'Teacher,' said John,* (one of the disciples) *'we saw a man driving out demons in your name and we told him to stop, because he was not one of us.'"* (Mark 9:38). The truth is that most people in Jesus' day believed in demon possession. They also believed some people were healers. More people went to the healers than to the primitive doctors, who often had a bad reputation, like the woman Jesus healed who had spent all her money on doctors (See Mark 5:26). The healing attributed to Jesus included fever, leprosy, bent back, deafness, paralysis, dropsy, blindness and a withered hand. Matthew, Mark and Luke record thirteen incidents of healing and six cases of exorcism.

There were two other Jewish healers who lived near the time of Jesus. One was Hanina ben Dosa of considerable fame who lived in Galilee about one generation after Jesus. He is credited with healing the son of the Jewish teacher Gamaliel. The second healer was Honi the circle drawer, who lived before Jesus in the middle of the first century BCE. He was especially famous for praying for rain. Once he prayed for rain and nothing happened. So he drew a circle and stood inside it and prayed to God that he would not move until God provided rain. There were a few drops. Honi then prayed again, saying that what he wanted was a whole lot more. It then rained so hard there was flooding.

Mark's gospel says Jesus healed many sick persons, then

charged them not to tell anyone. But in every case the healed person tells everyone. We wonder how a person healed of blindness could possible hide it from others. It may be that Jesus did not want to be overwhelmed by those who were curious or those who only wanted healing. Jesus had a message he wanted people to hear and accept.

Some students of medical anthropology see a distinction between curing a disease and healing an illness. While not completely accurate, we may say that an ill patient wants healing while his doctor wants to cure the disease. Very occasionally an ill person will complain because his doctor seems remote and detached from what he is going through. The doctor's focus is on the disease and what can be done to cure it. The patient carries with him a whole host of related concerns: how will the illness affect his job, will he be able to continue to work, will his daughter be able to complete college, what about the mortgage? Some Bible students say that Jesus may have been gifted as a healer of person's illnesses, but not one who could cure diseases. In a time when there were few, if any, cures for diseases, what Jesus had to offer may have been the best healing possible.

Bible Study Suggestions

Here are some suggestions to be followed in a productive use of the Bible. The first is to remember the Bible is always interpreted. Everyone who reads the Bible always interprets it, often in keeping with one's personal values. The person who believes warfare is a quick way to solve international problems will find many passages in the Old Testament in support of that view. The reader who opposes war will find many calls for peace, not the least from Jesus who said: "Love your enemies." We need to be aware of our human tendency to convert the Bible into our own social and political convictions.

The second suggestion grows out of the first, and that is to take seriously the teaching of Jesus. He taught that the Holy Spirit will lead individuals to the truth: *"The Advocate, the Holy Spirit, whom the Father will send in my name, will teach you everything, and remind you of all that I have said to you."* (John 14:26 NRSV). The ultimate authority for Christians is not the Bible, it is God the Holy Spirit, the third person of the Trinity.

Third is to remember that only God is God. The Bible must not be given an authority which is higher than the authority of the living God. Why not believe the Bible is in some sense both human and divine. If we can believe that Jesus was both human and divine, why not believe the same about the scripture? Is the Bible on a higher level than Jesus?

Fourth is to study the Bible and not simply read it. Why should we think the Bible or our religious faith should be easy? The simple fact is that the Bible is a demanding book, spanning thousands of years of human development. The customs and values of 5000 BCE to about 70 CE, which is the time period covered by the Bible, are quite different from ours today. Their experience of God can help us in our spiritual journey, but we need not adopt all their beliefs and practices. Openness to the Holy Spirit can help us see the difference.

Fifth, put yourself in the story. It is recommended that you underline or highlight the verses which are helpful and inspiring. The Protestant Reformers hoped the Bible would be available and read by every man and woman. Read so that your faith is influenced and informed as you read it. Try to identify your assumptions as you read. Ask "how does this apply to us, to me, today." The challenge of the Bible is to a life-long study. But don't make it too hard; you will never grasp it all, and you don't need to. Read looking for the help you need for living.

Finally, read and study Scripture with others who are also open to the guidance of the Spirit. Multitudes of people around the world meet together each week, in homes, not only to read and study the Scripture, but to care for and support one another.

This Is My Beloved Son

Chapter 10

DISCOVERING JESUS IN THE GOSPELS

In this chapter we take seriously a fact of history that the four Gospels were written a generation or longer after the crucifixion and resurrection of our Lord. Before they were written, the record of Jesus' teaching and ministry existed only in the memories of those people who had been with him and heard his words and observed his ministry. These memories were passed on to succeeding members of the Church. It is certain that nothing was written as events happened. Few could read and even fewer could write. We owe so much to those early Christians and their remarkable memories.

Every time the disciples and followers of Jesus met after the resurrection, they undoubtedly recalled the things he had said and done. Meanwhile, the church in Jerusalem continued to grow as we learn from the book of Acts, which also tells of the inclusion of Gentiles in the conversion of the family of Cornelius in chapter ten and especially in the mission work of the Apostle Paul and in the witness of Christians as they moved from place to place throughout the Roman Empire.

When the Jewish people in Jerusalem rebelled against Roman rule in 68-70 CE, the Jewish church in Jerusalem began to fade under the destructive impact of the war, while the Gentile Church continued to grow. It was during this time period, and later, that the four Gospels were written. It is probably true that all four Gospels were written by Gentile writers. Matthew's Gospel is the most Jewish, but it is not at all certain that the writer of Matthew was a Jew. The Gospels circulated for many years with no names attached.

To get this in perspective, most scholars believe the crucifixion and resurrection took place about the year 30 CE, though some believe it was 33 CE. As already noted, the first Gospel to be written was Mark in 65-75 CE. That would be 35 or 40 years after the resurrection, or about one generation. Although dates vary among scholars, it is generally believed that Matthew and Luke were written 80 to 90 CE, or 50 – 60 years after the resurrection, and John's gospel, 90 to 110 CE, or about 60 – 80 years after the resurrection of our Lord.

While we are grateful for the indispensable help the gospels give, we must recognize that in the long period of time before the gospels were written, some of the sayings and acts of Jesus could have been forgotten. We may also conclude from the dates that the gospels probably contain some conclusions and beliefs about Jesus which Christians came to embrace at the time Matthew, Mark, Luke and John were written, and therefore some elements do not go back to the time when Jesus lived and walked the hills of Galilee. Although not everyone agrees, it is probably true that not every saying in the Gospels credited to Jesus was actually spoken by him. Christians have always believed that Jesus is still alive and leading his church in every age. This means that new revelations from the "living Christ," given by a church member speaking "in the Spirit," might easily be confused with statements Jesus made when he taught the disciples and the crowds. Our task in this chapter is to discover the criteria needed to determine which sayings were probably spoken by the Lord during his time in Galilee and which were not. This will involve a careful and informed study and the end results cannot be guaranteed in every detail. A lot of patient work has already been done by scholars and students digging through the evidence in the gospels to recover our best knowledge of the Jesus the disciples knew and followed. Every serious student of the gospels must be ready to do the same.

There were other gospels in use by Christians in addition to the four in our New Testament. Some of these gospels survive today but are not part of the canon. Two which have garnered interest are the Infancy Gospel of James and the Gospel of Thomas.

The Infancy Gospel of James deals with the birth and childhood of Jesus. It is undoubtedly the creation of somebody's imagination. According to this gospel, when Jesus was a child, he did terrible things to his childhood friends, as he created one miracle after another, some harmful to his young playmates. The Gospel of Thomas is a Gnostic production, full of sayings presented as coming from Jesus. The basic belief of Gnosticism was that everything material or physical is evil, which meant that since the world is physical it is evil and must, therefore, have been created by an evil God, not the God of Jesus and Christians. They also believed there was a good God who sent Jesus to redeem the souls of people, but not their physical bodies, which are evil. Some Gnostics were sure Jesus did not exist in a physical body, but was entirely spiritual and therefore could not have been crucified. The person who died on the cross was not Jesus but another person who was somehow substituted in the place of Jesus, so that no one noticed. Needless to say, Gnosticism was eventually condemned by Christians as heresy, but it was very popular among some Christians for many years.

In 1945 the Gospel of Thomas was discovered in Egypt. It is not like the other gospels since there is none of the narrative material of Jesus' ministry, no miracles, healings or his birth, death or resurrection. It is a collection of teachings attributed to Jesus, presented in 114 sayings. While Thomas was not written until about 130 CE, it is believed some sayings are as early as the four gospels now in our New Testament. They do not, however, provide new material.

When we compare the gospels side by side we see that the same event in the ministry of Jesus is placed in a different position in the gospels. The Gospel of John reports that Jesus cleansed the Temple in his first visit to Jerusalem, while in Matthew, Mark and Luke, the cleansing took place during Jesus' only visit to the Holy City during the week he was crucified. The first three gospels tell us Jesus visited Jerusalem only once while in John, Jesus visited the Holy City often. It is possible that Jesus visited Jerusalem more than once since Matthew includes the following remark by Jesus when the Holy City came in view as he journeyed toward it, *"O Jerusalem, Jerusalem, How often have I desired to gather your children together as a hen gathers her brood under her wings, and you were not willing!"* (Matt 23:37 NRSV). If this was his first visit, why would he say he had often wanted to gather "your children" together? It may be that Jesus was speaking for God and not for himself.

Another challenge is the lack of context for the teachings and actions of Jesus. We would have a better understanding of events and teachings if we had the original context. An example of missing context is the decision of the Pharisees to join with the Herodians to "destroy" Jesus, as recorded in chapter three of Mark's gospel. This follows three very minor differences between Jesus and his critics, not enough to warrant plans to kill him. The first was the healing of a man with a withered hand on the Sabbath, which was not contrary to Mosaic Law. The second minor difference was when the disciples ate some grain on the Sabbath which they pulled from stalks in a grain field. Third was the criticism that Jesus' disciples did not fast like John the Baptist's disciples. The context for these unimportant offenses is entirely too weak to result in a conspiracy to kill Jesus. And yet, Mark 3:6 says, *"Then the Pharisees went out and began to plot with the Herodians how they might kill Jesus."* This plot may have happened later, but Mark puts it much too soon in his gospel. Also, it is not included in Matthew and Luke. (Question: What were the Pharisees doing walking in a grain field on the Sabbath when they criticized the disciples for stripping grain off and eating it?)

The headings above the first chapter of each gospel in today's New Testament says: "The Gospel according to," followed by the name Matthew, Mark, Luke or John. But according to early manuscript evidence, the gospels circulated without any titles or names for many years. Names began to appear about 175 CE, about one hundred years after the gospels were written. We have no clear explanation from history how the gospels finally received their titles, except for the Gospel of Luke. Whoever wrote the Gospel of Luke, also wrote the Book of Acts, as the opening verses of these two writings indicate. Luke, the physician, accompanied Paul on some of his missionary journeys, which may explain how his name was attached to the Gospel of Luke.

We have already noted some of the differences between the synoptic gospels, (Matthew, Mark and Luke), and John's gospel. Jesus performs many exorcisms in the synoptics, but in John's gospel there are none. In the synoptics, Jesus refuses to give a sign, or proof, that he speaks with God's authority, while in John there are many signs to prove Jesus' authority comes from God. In the synoptics, Jesus is reluctant to claim or even to accept titles of greatness, while in John, Jesus talks most of the time about himself and his intimate relationship with God. In the synoptics, Jesus' main subject is the kingdom of God, but in John, as we have already mentioned, it is found only twice, both times in Jesus' conversation with Nicodemus in chapter three. Jesus' teaching in the synoptics is often in short statements and parables; in John, there are no parables and Jesus talks at length, usually about his unique status with God. John's gospel contains the popular and helpful "I Am" sayings of Jesus: "I am the bread of life;" "I am the way, the truth and the life;" "I am the light of the world;" "I am the good shepherd;" "I am the resurrection and the life;" "I am in the Father and the Father is in me;" "I am the true vine, and my Father is the gardener;" "I am the vine; you are the branches." There are no "I am" statements in the first three gospels where Jesus never draws such attention to himself.

The writer of the Gospel of John was a leader of Christians for his time which was much later than the other gospels. We can be sure he wrote what he believed the living Christ had led him to put in his gospel. Where he departs from modern writing standards is that he has Jesus say things which were never spoken by the Jesus the disciples knew before the crucifixion. If an historian today was to have Abraham Lincoln say something which nobody ever heard him say, that historian would be roundly condemned. However, this sort of writing was largely accepted in the time of John's gospel. The Gospel of John has great value when we know what has happened and then accept his writing as a believer's gospel and embrace the truths which may have come from the living Christ, though not from the Jesus of history. John's gospel tells us that the living Christ still teaches his Church in the present, through the inner influence of the Holy Spirit.

While the Gospel of John has great value, the synoptic gospels are our main source of information about Jesus whom the disciples knew and loved. It must be recognized that the gospel writers allowed their imaginations to add to, rearrange and interpret the information about Jesus which they had in front of them when they wrote. It is possible to purchase a book called a synopsis, which arranges the three synoptic Gospels, Matthew, Mark and Luke, side by side. This allows the reader to compare how the Gospel writers have interpreted and arranged the same material. It is easy to see how one author places an incident or teaching of Jesus early in his record, while another author places the same material much later. Each writer felt free to arrange his gospel as he believed best. They were not working together and probably did not know each other since their gospels were written at different times and places. Of course, this makes it challenging to determine the correct order of events in Jesus' ministry, which most scholars are sure cannot be done with any certainty.

Jesus experienced first-hand the pain and suffering of his people who were caught in the impossible grip of the "domination system" of the Roman Empire. Aside from a few extremely wealthy people at the top, all others in the empire had someone who dominated or controlled them, and who, in turn, dominated or controlled other people under them. Peasants, artisans and the expendables, who were at the bottom of the human pyramid, had to struggle constantly just to hang on for one more day. About two-thirds of the annual crop of peasants went to support the upper classes. In a good year, they lived at a subsistence level, barely able to put food on the table, with enough seed left over for the next year's planting. A bad year could send them into sharecropping or worse.

A good way to proceed is to look for differences or possible contradictions in Jesus' recorded statements. He taught the benefit of forgiving, of settling disputes peace-fully, of praying for one's enemy, even loving enemies, which included the Romans. He said each person was salt of the earth and light of the world. He was sure people could rise to the highest level of living when they put their full trust and confidence in the Heavenly Father. He said God's love was so great that the very hairs of one's head were all numbered and known. He used the Heavenly Father as the example to follow in determining actions toward others. To value all people makes a person a true child of the God who sends God's sun and rain on evil people as well as the good because the Heavenly Father loves both. He was sure there was great rejoicing in Heaven when one troubled soul turns to God in hope. He encouraged people to trust God for every need, which would bring freedom from anxiety and care, enabling them to see God's goodness even in hard times. To shake off past habits and convictions and trust God for everything is what it means to live in the kingdom of God, which one can enter in the present moment. He demonstrated his good news in the way he lived, by daily accepting all kinds of people which greatly disturbed his critics who were appalled that he would not only welcome such people but actually eat with them. Because his message and style of living was upbeat, encouraging and positive, we can confidently conclude that any passages in the Gospels which depict Jesus as condemning and judgmental, must be carefully examined.

Following are some verses Jesus may not have spoken, since they do not compare favorably with the foregoing paragraph.

The quotation which follows is from a passage where Jesus is giving instructions to 70 disciples who were about to take the good news of the kingdom of God to Galilean villages and towns: *"He told them, 'The harvest is plentiful, but the workers are few. Ask the Lord of the harvest, therefore, to send out workers into his harvest field.'"* (Luke 10:2). But the same passage, also from Luke says, *"Woe to you, Chorazin! woe to you, Bethsaida! for if the mighty works done in you had been done in Tyre and Sidon, they would have repented long ago, sitting in sackcloth and ashes. But it shall be more tolerable in the judgment for Tyre and Sidon than for you. And you, Capernaum, will you be exalted to heaven? You shall be brought down to Hades."* (Luke 10:13-15). Did Jesus actually utter these words? How much of Jesus' message was aimed at towns or large groups, whether in wholesale salvation or condemnation? Would we be justified in saying "All Pittsburghers will be saved, but New Yorkers will be destroyed?" If whole cities are to be condemned, would that include only those who lived in those cities during Jesus' time or does it include all past time? And does it include the innocent persons as well as the guilty? Luke's woes simply do not sound like Jesus. The words are also out of place as part of the instructions Jesus was giving to his disciples when he sent them out with the good news. It appears obvious these two statements from Luke 10 do not belong together. They were surely inserted because the author felt they had to go somewhere. But did they ever come from Jesus?

Another statement by Jesus which has caused some concern is from Mark's gospel: *"If anyone causes one of these little ones who believe in me to sin, it would be better for him to be thrown into the sea with a large millstone tied around his neck. If your hand causes you to sin, cut it off. It is better for you to enter life maimed than with two hands to go into hell, where the fire never goes out."* (Mark 9:42-43). We know Jesus had great affection for children, although it is an extreme punishment to drown the offender in the sea. And who is to carry it out? This statement does not sound like the Lord. And it certainly does not sound like Jesus to encourage people to cut off sinful parts of the body to avoid spending eternity in hell. And does the evil reside in the body part or in the person? When the cutting is finished, will there be anything left? The quote from Mark sounds more like devoted Christians in the later Church who were having trouble winning and keeping converts. Many Christian preachers of more modern times have realized great success by dangling sinners over the flames of Hell. It is hard to believe Jesus would do that, although we know he could get quite angry. And his love for children is beyond dispute.

We are considering the pre-crucifixion Jesus which the disciples knew and were devoted to. We need to remember they "left everything" to follow Jesus. We recognize that the gospels tend to underrate these men. Mark especially has almost nothing good to say about them. When the disciples asked Jesus to explain the parable of the Sower, he gave them a critical response by saying, *"Don't you understand this parable? How then will you ever understand any parable?"* (Mark 4:13). When Jesus taught the crowd to see that it is not what goes into a person, but what comes out of a person which makes them unclean, he again berated the disciples: *"Are you so dull?"* he asked. (Mark 7:18).

Another time when Jesus warned them of the yeast of the Pharisees, meaning the teaching of the Pharisees, the disciples failed to understand. Then Jesus said, *"Do you have eyes but fail to see, and ears but fail to hear?"* (Mark 8:18). The question for today's Bible student is whether Jesus actually spoke so sharply to his disciples who gave up nearly everything to be with him and to learn from him. According to Luke 10:1ff, Jesus trusted them sufficiently to send the twelve and the seventy-two out on a mission to the towns which Jesus was about to enter. When they came back we are told *"the seventy-two returned with joy and said, 'Lord, even the demons submit to us in your name.' He* (Jesus) *replied, 'I saw Satan fall like lightning from heaven.'"* (Luke 10:17-18). Here Jesus is quite pleased with the performance of the disciples. Also note that Matthew and Luke are not nearly so critical of the disciples as Mark.

There are a number of nature miracles in the gospels, which seemed to have little impact on the disciples or the people. The stilling of the storm is found in all three synoptic gospels. Jesus and the disciples were crossing the sea when a sudden windstorm arose and the disciples were afraid the boat would sink. Jesus was asleep in the stern. When awakened, he rebuked the wind and there was a great calm. He also rebuked the disciples: *"Why are you so afraid? Do you still have no faith?"* (Mark 4:40). The disciples are filled with awe: *"Who is this? Even the wind and the waves obey him!"* (Mark 4:41).

The next nature miracle is the feeding of the 5,000 men through the multiplication of five loaves and two fish, also found in all three gospels. A great crowd is present. When it grows late, the disciples tell Jesus to dismiss the crowd so they can travel home in time for dinner. Jesus tells the disciples to feed them which they say they are unable to do. Jesus orders the disciples to have the people sit down on the grass in groups of fifty. Jesus then took the loaves and fish, gave thanks for them, and gave them to the disciples to give to the people. All were fed with twelve baskets of pieces left over.

The feeding is immediately followed by the miracle of Jesus walking on water, found in Matthew and Mark. Jesus had the disciples get in the boat and cross over to the other side while he dismissed the crowd and went up into a mountain to pray. The disciples are making very little progress in the boat because of strong headwinds. Early in the morning, Jesus came to them walking on the water. Only Matthew says that Peter asks permission from Jesus to walk to him on the water. He is able to do so until he gives way to fear and begins to sink. Jesus rescues him saying, *"You of little faith, why did you doubt?"* (Matt 14:31). Mark says the wind ceased when they got back in the boat. Mark adds, *"They were completely amazed, for they had not understood about the loaves; their hearts were hardened."* (Mark 6:51-52). Mark seems to be saying that even though they had experienced the miracle of the feeding of the five thousand, it had not increased their faith. Either Satan had hardened their hearts or they were simply not greatly impressed.

The next miracle is the feeding of the four thousand. Jesus returned from the district of Tyre and Sidon to a mountain near the Sea of Galilee. A great crowd quickly assembled with their sick and lame to be healed. After three days, Jesus is concerned because the people have no food. The disciples again do not know what to do, but they do have seven loaves and a few small fish. Jesus gave a blessing, broke the loaves and fish, and gave the pieces to the disciples who gave them to the people. Seven baskets were left over and four thousand men were fed, not counting women and children.

When the disciples were worried about not bringing enough

bread along, Jesus asked them how many baskets of food were left over from the feeding of the five thousand and the four thousand and they remember. Jesus cannot understand how they can be concerned about having enough bread when they have witnessed the miracles of feeding five and then four thousand men, not counting women and children. The miracles did not produce faith in the disciples and there is no indication that the crowds were impressed either. But do all these miracles in the gospels produce faith in people today?

After the first feeding the gospels say of the crowd only that *"they all ate and were satisfied."* After the four thousand it says only, *"They ate and were filled."* There is no indication that anyone was won over to discipleship. We recognize that the miracles were included to convey a comforting truth, even though they may not have actually happened. When Jesus stilled the storm on the sea, the result is reassurance to those who are facing a storm of issues or crises in their personal lives. Whether it actually happened is not as important as the help received when the suffering individual turns to Jesus in a personal storm.

Next we consider the birth stories found in Matthew and Luke, but not in Mark or John. Why were these stories included, since there is no reference to them in the rest of the New Testament? Evidence shows that belief in a virgin birth developed much later in the life of the Church, in time to be included in these two gospels. After the deaths of many great men in antiquity they were declared to be virgin born. Alexander the Great was one. Were some Christians in the infant church trying to keep up with pagan practices? Note that in Matthew and Luke, Joseph had nothing to do with Jesus' birth, and yet both gospels trace Jesus' genealogy through Joseph and not through Mary. It is especially confusing since Matthew, Luke and John say that Jesus was "the son of Joseph" or "the carpenter's son."

The early Christians diligently searched the Old Testament for predictions believed to be fulfilled in Jesus. Bethlehem was understood to be the birthplace of the Messiah, based on Micah 5:2: *"But you, Bethlehem Ephrathah, though you are small among the clans of Judah, out of you will come for me one who will be ruler over Israel, whose origins are from of old, from ancient times."* (Micah 5:2). Based on this prophecy, which may or may not have applied to the coming Messiah, Matthew and Luke believed it did, and so had to find a way to have Jesus born in Bethlehem. Also Matthew, but not Luke, reports the flight of the holy family to Egypt, in fulfillment of Hosea 11:1 NRSV: *"When Israel was a child, I loved him, and out of Egypt I called my son."* This is clearly a reference to the nation Israel and its deliverance from bondage in Egypt and was not a prophecy relating to the infant Jesus. "My son" is a collective reference to the Israelite people. It appears Matthew chose to see "my son" as referring to Jesus as the divine Son of God, something which Jesus never claimed for himself in the synoptic gospels. In fact, Jesus never claimed titles for himself in the first three gospels. When Peter declared Jesus to be the Messiah, at Caesarea-Philippi, Jesus immediately told the disciples not to tell anyone. We may assume that Jesus did not want his followers declaring him to be the Messiah, which would put his mission and his safety in jeopardy. But did Jesus himself believe he was the Messiah? He does not make that claim in the synoptics, although it is on nearly every page of John's gospel.

All Jews were considered to be "Sons of God," which included women in this all-encompassing term. Paul says in Romans that *"all who are led by the Spirit of God are sons of God."* (Romans 8:14). Paul writes nearly the same in Galatians: *"Because you are sons, God sent the Spirit of his Son into our hearts, the Spirit who calls out, 'Abba, Father.'"* (Gal 4:6). Jesus said his audience could become sons of God: *"Love your enemies and pray for those who persecute you, that you may be sons of your Father in heaven."* (Matt 5:44-45 RSV). We might say that Jesus was a special Son of God among the sons of God. The church later decided that Jesus could not be half deity and half human; he was somehow both, fully human and fully deity. The Jesus the disciples knew was thoroughly human. In Jesus' time, there was no clear understanding of Messiah, Son of Man or Son of God among

Jewish people.

According to Matthew, the virgin birth of Jesus was in fulfillment of the prophecy of Isaiah 7:14, which constitutes a misreading of the prophet's warning. Matthew quotes the prophecy as follows: *"The virgin will be with child and will give birth to a son, and they will call him 'Immanuel,' which means, 'God with us.'"* (Matt 1:23). However, an unbiased reading of Isaiah's prophecy gives a very different understanding. Isaiah was trying to persuade Ahaz, the King of Judah, to trust in God and not to appeal for help from the Assyrian Emperor. Judah was under attack from the combined armies of Syria and the northern kingdom of Israel. When King Ahaz refused to take Isaiah's advice, Isaiah pronounced a prophecy of doom with these opening words, *"The virgin will be with child and will give birth to a son, and will call him Immanuel."* (Isaiah 7:14). Had Matthew read more in the prophecy of Isaiah, he would have known that Isaiah's words did not apply to the birth of Jesus. Isaiah went on to say that before the child to be born of "the virgin" (or young woman) grows to maturity, both the Kingdoms of Syria and Israel would be devastated, which is why King Ahaz should have simply trusted in God. God will indeed be Immanuel, "God with Ahaz," not in comfort, but in judgment, for not accepting Isaiah's word from God. The Hebrew word for virgin is "almah," which refers to a young virgin, just married, but not yet pregnant with her first child. Matthew snatched a verse from the Old Testament and forced it to mean what he wanted it to mean.

Luke does not refer to Isaiah, but still says it was a virginal conception, except by the power of God: *"The Holy Spirit will come upon you, and the power of the Most High will overshadow you. So the holy one to be born will be called the Son of God."* (Luke 1:35). It is helpful to recall that in Jewish usage "Son of God" does not mean "more than human," although that is probably what Luke intended it to mean: that Jesus was deity, God in human flesh.

Luke also says that Jesus was born when Quirinius was Governor of Syria. We know from reliable historical information that Quirinius was governor of Syria in 6 CE. But Luke also dates the birth of John the Baptist and Jesus when Herod the Great was still alive. Since Herod died in 4 BCE, Quirinius could not have been governor when Jesus was born. In reality, it is easier to date past events using information available to us today, than it was in Luke's time. They did not have calendars or a dating system such as we have today. This is a blow to many Christians who appear to stake their salvation on the belief that the Bible was 'dictated' by God and is totally without error. If so, how could God have made such a serious mistake in dating the birth of Jesus? It was the human writers who made the mistake, not God.

What can we conclude from the above? First, it is obvious that Old Testament prophecies were used to build the story of Jesus' birth, even though they had little or nothing to do with historic facts. Why does Matthew say *"Isn't this the carpenter's son?"* And why does Luke say, *"Isn't this Joseph's son?"* (Luke 4:22). And from John's gospel, *"They said, 'Is this not Jesus, the son of Joseph, whose father and mother we know?'"* (John 6:42 NRSV). How could the gospels say Joseph had nothing to do with Jesus' birth but also declare he was the son of Joseph? We also know that in the first and second centuries, when the virgin birth of Jesus was believed by most Christians, a rumor circulated for decades among critics of the Christian movement, that Mary had been impregnated by a Roman soldier named Panthera.

Time after time, the writers of the synoptic gospels, especially Matthew, found a prophecy which they believed applied to Jesus and then created an event to fit the prophecy. However, the early Christians were certainly correct in their use of some of the prophecies, especially in the 53rd chapter of Isaiah which amazingly applies to much that was true in Jesus' life. Here are a few verses from this amazing chapter: *"He was despised and rejected by men, a man of sorrows, and familiar with suffering. Like one from whom men hide their faces he was despised, and we esteemed him not. Surely he took up our infirmities and carried our sorrows, yet we considered him stricken by God, smitten by him, and afflicted. But he was pierced for our transgressions, he was crushed for our iniquities; the punishment that brought us peace was upon him, and by his wounds we are healed."* (Isaiah 53:3-5). This suffering servant of Isaiah has always presented a challenge to both Jewish and Christian scholars.

By the time the gospels were written, the church was largely Gentile and had already suffered persecution from the Roman government. We also have reliable evidence that just ten years after the resurrection, a few Christians were already living in Rome. As noted earlier, Christians were blamed by emperor Nero for the fire which destroyed much of the city of Rome with an untold number of believers cruelly killed. This was in 60 CE, only about 30 years after the resurrection of Jesus.

The gospels were written 40 to 80 years after the crucifixion. Nearly all Bible scholars agree that Mark's gospel was the first to be written, about 65-75 CE. It may have been circulated at the time the Romans succeeded in utterly defeating the Jewish people of the Holy Land who had rebelled against Roman tyranny, 68-70 CE. There was simmering anger throughout the empire directed against Jews for daring to rebel against Roman rule. Unfortunately, all of the four gospels direct this anger at the Jewish people instead of the High Priest and the Roman governor, Pilate, who was known for his cruelty and who alone ordered the crucifixion of Jesus.

This leads us to one of the saddest features of the four gospels. Governor Pilate is a good example of how the gospels turned the spotlight of guilt for Jesus' death on the Jews and not on the Romans and the Jewish High Priest group where it belonged. Pilate was a vicious man who committed many atrocities in his ten year rule. His disruptive way of ruling caused so much trouble that the emperor eventually decided that he could no longer be used. The Jewish philosopher and statesman Philo, a contemporary of Pilate, wrote about the governor's "briberies, insults, robberies, outrages and wanton injuries, the executions without trial constantly repeated and supremely grievous cruelty" that marked Pilate's rule. And yet, when Jesus was on trial before Pilate, the governor is portrayed in the gospels as a man of the highest justice who tried repeatedly to let Jesus go free.

In Luke's gospel, Pilate said to the Chief Priests: *"You brought me this man as one who was perverting the people; and here, I have examined him in your presence, and have not found this man guilty of any of your charges against him...Indeed he has done nothing to deserve death. I will therefore have him flogged and released."* (Luke 23:14). Because of the unceasing demand of "the crowd," Pilate reluctantly condemned Jesus to be crucified according to Luke's gospel. This is not history; it is a sad attempt by Luke to place the blame, not on the Romans, but on the Jews. To blame Pilate and the Romans for Jesus' crucifixion would have put the infant Christian church scattered throughout the empire under suspicion, facing the outrage of the Roman people. While understandable, it later brought great pain and suffering to thousands of Jews at the hands of the established Christian Church.

Matthew's gospel agrees with Luke, that Pilate tried valiantly to have Jesus released. Even Pilate's wife interceded for Jesus. Matthew records that Pilate went so far as to wash his hands saying, *"I am innocent of this man's blood; see to it yourselves."* To this the crowd, led by the High Priest, shouted, *"His blood be on us and on our children."* Here we must pause and reflect sorrowfully on the hundreds of Jews in later centuries who were persecuted, tortured with unspeakable cruelty and killed in the Church's Inquisition, as a result of these sinful words, "His blood be on us and on our children." Should these Scriptures ever be read during Lent without due recognition of the pain they later caused innocent fellow humans?

The Gospel of Mark, the first to be written, found a unique way to place the blame on the Jews for the death of Jesus. Mark's author includes something which no historian has been able to verify: that each year at Passover, Pilate would show a side of his character which appears nowhere else by releasing a condemned criminal to win the approval of the populace. In this case Mark says he offered to release a man named Barabbas who committed murder in an insurrection attempt to overthrow the Romans. Historians tell us there is no way Pilate would release anyone who had rebelled against Roman rule. However, in Mark's account, the

High Priest's loud crowd demanded the release of Barabbas and the crucifixion of Jesus. In Mark 15:10 we are told that Pilate *"realized that it was out of jealousy that the chief priest had handed him* (Jesus) *over."* In verse 14 *"Pilate asked them, 'Why, what evil has he done?'"* Finally in verse 15, Pilate capitulates to the demands of the High Priest and *"wishing to satisfy the crowd, released Barabbas for them; and after flogging Jesus, he handed him over to be crucified."* Like Matthew, Mark agrees it was the Jews, led by the High Priest's "crowd," who were responsible for the death of Jesus. This too, added to the pain and suffering of Jews at the hands of Christians in later years.

The same Barabbas incident is found in Luke's gospel where Pilate tries to have Jesus released after flogging him, but without success. In Luke 23:23, the High Priest's crowd *"kept urgently demanding with loud shouts that he should be crucified; and their voices prevailed. So Pilate gave his verdict that their demand should be granted."* Poor Pilate didn't want to crucify Jesus. But he did.

The Gospel of John also puts the blame for Jesus' crucifixion on the Jews rather than on the Romans and the High Priest where it belonged. Throughout his gospel, John constantly fails to differentiate between the Jewish leaders and the Jewish people. The term "the Jews" occurs 67 times in the King James Version of John's gospel and 57 times in the New International Version. When Jesus appeared before Pilate, the governor repeatedly referred to the crowd as "the Jews." He also seems to taunt the crowd by referring to Jesus as "The King of the Jews," an accusation the High Priest charged against Jesus. However, the true identity of the crowd which called for Jesus' death is seen in the event which immediately preceded the trial before Pilate, as found in John 18:28 NRSV: *"Then they took Jesus from Caiaphas to Pilate's headquarters."* Caiaphas was the High Priest who appears to have presided over the "trial" of Jesus before the High Priest Council. They had already reached the verdict that Jesus must be executed. So they turned him over to Pilate with the recommendation that he be executed. As it happened in the other gospels, John's gospel says Pilate did not want to condemn Jesus. He also offered to release Jesus instead of Barabbas, but "the Jews" shouted for the release of Barabbas. After trying again, Pilate yielded to their demands, but with a surprising outcome, for the governor, *"handed him over to them to be crucified, so they took Jesus and, carrying the cross by himself, he went out to The Place of the Skull...There they crucified him."* (John 19:16-18). The author of John certainly gives the impression that it was not the Romans but "the Jews" who crucified Jesus, for it clearly says that Pilate handed Jesus "over to them to be crucified."

The gospels rightly tell us it was the High Priest group who condemned Jesus and then handed him over to Pilate for execution who, without hesitation, ordered his crucifixion. This is what the gospels should have reported. It is not difficult to understand why the gospels exonerated Pilate while blaming the Jewish people since Christians in many parts of the Roman world faced a hard task explaining how the person they claimed as Lord and Savior of the world could have been executed by the Romans. We also need to remember that the gospels were written after the Jewish people rebelled against the Romans in 68 – 70 CE, with most citizens of the empire angry at the Jews for daring to rebel.

Before leaving this section, we repeat that the Romans held the High Priest responsible for maintaining peace, especially during festival occasions, when thousands of Jewish worshippers crowded the city of Jerusalem. The High Priest knew if he did not stop troubling incidents before they got out of hand, the Romans would do what they had done before and Roman soldiers would be turned loose on the populace with many innocent Jews killed. While there is no evidence that Jesus was any threat to the peace of Jerusalem, the High Priest saw an opportunity to have Jesus silenced along with his disturbing views on religion, including his attitude toward the Temple. So the High Priest simply told Pilate that Jesus was a dangerous upstart and Pilate did the rest.

Chapter 11

WHY WAS JESUS CRUCIFIED?

It was the High Priest who handed Jesus over to Pilate with the charge that he was a source of trouble, and Pilate quickly ordered his scourging and crucifixion. The High Priest knew a lot about Jesus and did not like what he had learned. To the High Priest group, Jesus was an upstart peasant from Galilee, who appeared to be determined to change too many traditions of Jewish life and worship. And he was much too popular among the masses who were always ready to grumble and complain about the heavy Temple burdens they had to carry as compared to the wealthy elite. Added to this was the action of Jesus in physically disrupting the selling of sacrifices and the exchange of currency into the coins used in the Temple. Images stamped on the coins were not allowed in the Temple. Coins which the pilgrims brought with them were always stamped with an image, usually of the emperor. This exchange of currency had been in use for many years. After the "cleansing of the Temple," all the priestly efforts to stop Jesus or to embarrass him in front of the people failed according to the Gospel accounts. So the High Priest concluded that he must be silenced. But apparently under Roman rule, they did not have the power to execute, so they turned him over to Pilate, who knew exactly what to do with a mere peasant.

But there was even more which contributed to Jesus' condemnation. The God of fierce anger and wrathful judgment found in some places in the Old Testament, found little or no room in Jesus' teaching. This is important since it was one reason why some of the Jewish leaders of his people rejected him. Several times in the gospels Jesus identified the Scribes and the Pharisees as the principal groups which criticized his message and his actions. Not all of them were critical, since Jesus had supporters and friends among these two groups. Most of his critics were making a valiant effort to do everything in their power to be good Jews by living up to their understanding of the demands of God for holiness and purity. But Jesus believed some went too far, especially in their rejection of people who simply did not have it in their power to live up to such high standards.

Because of their belief in the wrath of God, some could not accept Jesus' portrayal of God as compassionate and forgiving. After all, they were making every effort to please God, so how could they be content with a God who accepts people who were not trying as hard as they? Too many people were not even making an effort to live up to the purity regulations, the tithing demands and Sabbath limitations. How could Jesus as a religious teacher dismiss these cherished interpretations of the Torah? How could Jesus preach that the God of the Law of Moses accepts people who didn't try hard enough or didn't even try? To say Jesus saw God as accepting those whom others regarded as unacceptable is clearly found in much of his teaching. This feature of the Lord's message contributed to his eventual rejection by people of power.

A closely related element in Jesus' teaching had to do with his understanding of the kingdom of God. The part which his critics could not accept had to do with the qualifications of the people accepted into God's kingdom. His critics set very high religious standards, but Jesus clearly taught that the love of God was freely given to everyone and that all who put the compassionate God at the center of personal thinking and acting was accepted in God's kingdom. Since nearly all of Jesus' teaching had to do with some aspect of the kingdom of God, this was a constant irritant to the religious elite and other powerful leaders of the people. When Jesus was criticized by the Chief Priests and Elders in the Temple, he ended the conversation with these words, *"Truly I tell you, the tax collectors and the prostitutes are going into the kingdom of God ahead of you."* (Matt 21:31 NRSV). To people of power and religious attainment, this was too much. These same people were especially critical because Jesus not only delighted in spending time with the wrong people, but, they said, he even eats with tax collectors, sinners and outcasts. We find this in an amazing statement found in Luke 15:2: *"The Pharisees and the scribes murmured, saying, 'This man welcomes sinners, and eats with them.'"* While Jesus cared for all people, his chief concern was for those at the bottom of society, those having the hardest time making it in life.

There are numerous examples of Jesus spending time and eating with those whom the super religious regarded as unacceptable. One example happened right after Jesus called the tax collector Matthew to be one of his disciples. While Jesus was having dinner at Matthew's house, many tax collectors and "sinners" came and ate with him and his disciples. When the Pharisees saw this, they asked his disciples, *"'Why does your teacher eat with tax collectors and sinners?' On hearing this, Jesus said, 'It is not the healthy who need a doctor, but the sick. But go and learn what this means: I desire mercy, not sacrifice. For I have not come to call the righteous, but sinners.'"* (Matt 9:10).

Jesus would have at least one meal every day as he traveled from place to place in Galilee. We are told that crowds were always present, which surely would have occasionally included mealtimes. Did Jesus welcome all present to join in the meal and share whatever they had? And would it not be like Jesus to assume the role of host, with the prayer and free conversation? When we consider the frequent mention of joy in Jesus' ministry, we can be reasonably certain that these mealtimes, which upset his critics, were times of joyful celebration for Jesus and his friends.

Jesus was certain that the needs of people come first with God and because he was sure of this, he healed on the Sabbath day. This greatly inflamed some who had life divided into a long list of acceptable and unacceptable Sabbath behaviors, all based on this Commandment: *"Remember the Sabbath day by keeping it holy. Six days you shall labor and do all your work, but the seventh day is a Sabbath to the LORD your God. On it you shall not do any work, neither you, nor your son or daughter, nor your manservant or maidservant, nor your animals, nor the alien within your gates. "* (Ex 20:8-10). Not only was Jesus criticized for healing the sick on the Sabbath, but he also walked too far on the Sabbath, and his disciples stripped grain off the stalks on the Sabbath and ate it. Not only did Jesus reject the criticism of his critics, but what does his attitude toward the Sabbath tell us about his interpretation of the Sabbath Law established by Moses? Was he not free to interpret the Law in a new and more compassionate way?

Another action of Jesus which greatly disturbed some of the powerful and contributed to his condemnation was the way he freely announced the forgiveness of sins. His adversaries believed that to announce forgiveness was assuming a power which belonged only to God. We can be sure that Jesus sometimes announced forgiveness because he knew that many of his people carried the double burden of their illness and the belief that sickness was God's punishment for sins which the sick person was believed to have committed. Jesus did not want people to bear that added and unnecessary burden. He knew his compassionate Heavenly Father did not want his children to suffer under a load of guilt, real or imagined. Forgiveness is a given, and cannot be earned by any works of good behavior. God's forgiveness is to be accepted and celebrated with thanksgiving. Apparently Jesus believed this understanding of God's unwavering love was more likely to lead to spiritual and moral growth in the individual. But it also contributed to his death.

And then there was Jesus' joy which, strangely enough, was also a factor in his rejection. This feature of Jesus' personality is often missed. There was a drawing of Jesus which circulated for years in the early centuries which showed him unsmiling and sad with this inscription underneath, "He never smiled." Too often he has been depicted as serious, demanding and difficult. And yet it must have been a joyful and happy experience to spend time with Jesus. We can see this emphasis on joy in his teaching about the kingdom of God. Jesus said that living under God's compassionate rule was like the joy of finding a pearl of great worth, like the delight of finding a treasure in a field, which he presented in a double parable: *"The kingdom of heaven is like treasure hidden in a field, which someone found and hid; then in his joy he goes and sells all that he has and buys that field. Again, the kingdom of heaven is like a merchant in search of fine pearls; on finding one pearl of great value, he went and sold all that he had and bought it."* (Matt 13:44-46). In Jesus' view, life in the kingdom is a thing of joy because God is accepting, encouraging and generous, whose compassion never ceases.

He said he had good news for the poor who are often forgotten, but who are much quicker than the rich in seeing their need for God. Entering the kingdom is allowing God to have the central place in one's life. It is so good it is worth every sacrifice. In Chapter 3 of John's gospel we are told that Jesus' first miracle had to do with keeping a wedding celebration going. From this we may conclude that life in the kingdom of God is like a wedding, which was the most carefree and happy experience of his overburdened people. In God's kingdom, life is a party with singing, feasting and dancing, despite the difficult experiences which have always been a part of human existence.

Another action of Jesus which disturbed some, especially men, was his natural way of accepting women into his fellowship and ministry as mentioned earlier. We are told in Luke 8:1-3 that there was a group of women who not only accompanied Jesus at times in his travels, but supplied some of his needs and those of his disciples, "...out of their resources." These and other women followed Jesus to Jerusalem on his last journey to the Holy City. And they were present near the cross when Jesus was crucified. It was women who were first to go to the tomb on Easter Sunday.

At least one was a woman of the streets. We find the account in the gospel of Luke *"...a woman of the city, who was a sinner,* (prostitute) *having learned that he was eating in the Pharisee's house, brought an alabaster jar of ointment. She stood behind him at his feet, weeping, and began to bathe his feet with her tears and to dry them with her hair. Then she continued kissing his feet and anointing them with the ointment."* (Luke 7:37,38 NRSV) This woman had undoubtedly heard Jesus speaking about the kindness, compassion and acceptance of God and had observed it in the way Jesus honored all kinds of people. Out of gratitude for this degree of hope and the encouragement she felt which came from knowing that someone understood her plight, she took this action to express her affectionate appreciation. She may have been one of many women forced into prostitution by a husband who simply got tired of her and divorced her, which was allowed by the Mosaic Law, while women could not divorce. If she had no family to go back to, the only means of support open to her was the oldest profession of humankind. She may have had children in her care also. Jesus felt deep compassion for such people, a compassion which was rooted in the great heart of God. But not everyone agreed. It takes little imagination to conclude that some were so angry over his compassionate treatment of women they wanted Jesus silenced. To these men, Jesus' acceptance of women directly threatened the Mosaic teaching that every woman must be under the authority of a man - a father, husband, brother, etc. It is very close to the thing we find in Saudi Arabia where women are never to be seen in public without a male relative present.

Jesus' audience and critics were not confined to Galilee. Matthew tells us that *"great crowds from Galilee, Decapolis, Jerusalem, Judea and from beyond the Jordan followed him."* (Mt 4:25). In other words, he was well known and popular over a large area. More significantly, Matthew 15:1 RSV tells us that "Pharisees and Scribes came to Jesus from Jerusalem," probably to evaluate his actions and to add their voices to that of his local critics. Clearly, the majority of the people who heard Jesus would never have lifted their voices to end his life. His critics, especially among the Scribes, Pharisees and the High Priest class, do bear responsibility for Jesus' death. The High Priest in Jerusalem and his advisers are most responsible, having recommended to Pilate that Jesus be executed. We need always to remember that it was Governor Pilate, and not "the Jews," who condemned Jesus to death by crucifixion.

Chapter 12

RESURRECTION

Exactly what happened after the crucifixion is impossible to establish, except that God had the last word and not the High Priest or Rome. In Mark's last chapter, we read that Mary Magdalene, Mary the mother of James, and Salome took spices to anoint Jesus' body very early on Easter Sunday. They were worried about who would roll the stone away at the entrance of the tomb. When they arrived, the stone was already removed and inside was a young man in a white robe who said, *"Don't be alarmed. You are looking for Jesus the Nazarene, who was crucified. He has risen! He is not here. See the place where they laid him. But go, tell his disciples and Peter, 'He is going ahead of you into Galilee. There you will see him, just as he told you.'"* (Mark 16:6-7). The experience frightened the women so greatly they told no one what had happened. Mark's Gospel abruptly ends at this point, though two improved endings to the chapter were supplied at a later date.

Matthew's account is different. Matthew says when Mary Magdalene and the "other Mary" arrived at the tomb there was an earthquake, an angel descended and rolled the stone away from the entrance of the tomb. The Roman guards were frozen with fear. The angel told the women to inform the disciples that Jesus had gone ahead to Galilee and they would meet him there. Then Jesus himself appeared to the women and repeated the angel's message. Matthew's account ends with the great commission in chapter 28.

In Luke's account, we are told "the women" went to the tomb and found it empty. Then two men in gleaming clothes appeared beside them and said, *"Why do you look for the living among the dead? He is not here; he has risen!"* (Luke 24:5-6 NRSV). The women are identified as *"Mary Magdalene, Joanna, Mary the mother of James, and the others."* (Luke 24:10). The women returned and reported their experience to the disciples, who did not believe them. Peter then ran to the tomb but saw only that it was empty. Luke then includes the account of the two believers on the way to Emmaus when Jesus joined them, but they failed to recognize him. Upon reaching their destination, they invited Jesus, still unrecognized, to spend the night with them. When they sat down to eat, Jesus became the host, took the bread and broke it. Then they recognized him and he disappeared. The two quickly returned to Jerusalem to tell the others, only to learn that the risen Jesus had appeared to Peter. Then Jesus appeared among them and said, "Peace be with you." He then ate some fish and told them to wait in Jerusalem until they were "clothed with power from on high." Jesus and the others then went to a place near Bethany where he ascended into Heaven. That is Luke's record of what happened.

The book of Acts, also written by Luke, gives us a very different account than we find in Luke's gospel. In Acts, Jesus was with the disciples off and on for forty days, meeting with them often, apparently eating meals with them regularly and frequently talking about the kingdom of God. He instructed them to remain in Jerusalem until they were "baptized with the Holy Spirit." The disciples ask an odd question: was Jesus about to restore the kingdom to Israel, which sounds like they wanted to know if Jesus was somehow going to get rid of the Romans and establish Israel's independence. Jesus gently told them it was not for them to know; their job was to witness to the Lord in Jerusalem and to the ends of the earth. Having said this, he ascended into Heaven. An angel then appeared and told them Jesus would return in the same way he departed.

John's gospel appears to have two endings. The first in chapter 20 concludes with these words: *"Jesus did many other miraculous signs in the presence of his disciples, which are not recorded in this book. But these are written that you may believe that Jesus is the Christ, the Son of God, and that by believing you may have life in his name."* (John 20:30-31). But in the next chapter, Peter and some of the disciples are by the Sea of Tiberius when Peter suddenly says "I am going fishing." They fish all night and catch nothing. At daybreak they see Jesus on the shore but do not recognize him. He instructs them to cast their nets on the right side of the boat with the result they are unable to get all the fish into the boat. Then the unnamed "disciple whom Jesus loved" tells Peter it is the Lord. When they come ashore, they see Jesus has prepared a fire with cooked fish and bread which he gives to them. Jesus asks Peter three times, "Do you love me?" Peter responds positively each time, "Yes, Lord, you know that I love you," and Jesus says "Feed my lambs." Peter asks about the disciple whom Jesus loved and Jesus' reply sounds like the beloved disciple will never die: *"If I want him to remain alive until I return, what is that to you? You must follow me."* (John 21:22). The ending of the chapter seems to say that the unnamed beloved disciple is the author of the Gospel of John, or the one who supplied the accurate information for the gospel: *"This is the disciple who testifies to these things and who wrote them down. We know that his testimony is true."* (John 21:24).

The earliest account of the resurrection comes from Paul in I Corinthians, who says Jesus *"appeared to Peter, and then to the Twelve. After that, he appeared to more than five hundred of the brothers at the same time, most of whom are still living, though some have fallen asleep."* (I Corinthians 15:5-8). Note that Paul does not include appearances to women. There is no mention of an appearance to "five hundred brothers" in any other part of the New Testament.

Paul often defended his experience of the resurrected Christ which occurred on the road to Damascus when he was converted. He insisted that the resurrected Jesus had a spiritual body and that believers will also have a spiritual body in heaven.

Since we cannot reconstruct exactly what happened when Jesus was resurrected, it becomes a matter for faith and trust. To use faith is not a cop-out; it is simply leaving things which are beyond us in the hands of God. While the first Christians had differing experiences of the resurrected Christ, they were willing to die holding on to that great experience, absolutely convinced he was alive and with them. There is no reason to doubt they truly experienced Jesus after the crucifixion. It is also true that Christians one hundred and even two thousand years after the resurrection are sure they have also experienced the living Lord.

Meanwhile each Christian has a personal calling from the resurrected Jesus: *"All authority in heaven and on earth has been given to me. Go therefore and make disciples of all nations, baptizing them in the name of the Father and of the Son and of the Holy Spirit, and teaching them to obey everything that I have commanded you. And remember, I am with you always, to the end of the age."* (Matt 28:18-20)

Chapter 13

WOMEN IN THE CHURCH

In this chapter we focus more on the importance of women in Jesus' ministry and in the early decades of the church. A few scholars are convinced that some women worked as apostles to spread everywhere the good news of God's love. An apostle is "one who is sent," and women were often said to be present with men when there was a sending forth. In chapter 24 of Luke's gospel, the risen Christ appeared to a group of believers which undoubtedly included women. He commissioned them in verse 48: *"You are witnesses of these things. I am going to send you what my Father has promised; but stay in the city until you have been clothed with power from on high."*

In Acts chapter one, also written by Luke, he tells us that a group of Christians were meeting in an upper room in Jerusalem. Women were present: *"They all joined together constantly in prayer, along with the women and Mary the mother of Jesus, and with his brothers."* (Acts 1:14). The next verse says the number of people in the upper room was 120. On the day of Pentecost they were together when the Holy Spirit descended on them and each one spoke in tongues: *"All of them were filled with the Holy Spirit and began to speak in other tongues as the Spirit enabled them."* (Acts 2:4). There is nothing to indicate that only men spoke in tongues, although it is true that in Peter's speech to the crowd which gathered, he refers to the tongues speakers as "these men." That is the usual form of address. Peter then quotes the prophet Joel who wrote that in the last days *"your sons and your daughters will prophesy."* (Joel 2:28). Joel included women. We can only conclude that women were "sent" as surely as men.

Jesus lived in a male-dominated, patriarchal world with rigid boundaries between men and women. Probably all of the books of the Bible, both Old and New Testaments, were written by men and from the male viewpoint. While the "good wife" of Proverbs 33 is highly extolled, women were very much subordinate. And if you look carefully at all the tasks this "good wife" of Proverbs accomplished day and night, you will see that her husband has little to do but sit all day with the "elders" at the gate of the city. A prayer, reported to be repeated at every synagogue meeting at one point in history, said, "O God, I thank Thee that I was not born a woman." When you see how hard Proverbs says wives had to work, you can understand why a man would not want to be a woman.

So how did Jesus' critics react when they saw women among the disciples and friends of the Lord? As noted earlier, Jesus' acceptance of women and children flowed directly out of his experience of the compassionate and accepting Heavenly Father, who loves and cares for all his children, male and female, young and old.

Jesus' acceptance of women continued in the church for only a few years. It was eventually set aside in favor of the leadership and dominance of men. The Apostle Paul wrote: *"As in all the congregations of the saints, women should remain silent in the churches. They are not allowed to speak, but must be in submission, as the Law says."* (1 Cor. 14:33-34). Strange that Paul should speak of the Law since he was the Apostle to the Gentiles whose argument was that Gentiles did not need to submit to the Law. Why does he resort to the Law to keep women in their place?

It is true that Paul calls for the submission of women in the passage above and again in Ephesians 5:22-24. However, some scholars suspect that these passages may have been added by a later copyist who felt Paul's letters needed to be updated to current thinking in the church regarding the place of women.

Some scholars wonder why only one name, Cleopas, is given for the two Emmaus disciples. If it was two men traveling together, or if it was a husband and wife, we would expect both names to appear. Could it have been a woman who was not married to Cleopas? Could it have been two followers of Jesus who were liberated by his radical equality so that they felt free to travel together, giving the appearance to strangers that they were husband and wife? The woman could not travel alone, but she may have been free to travel with a man even though they were not married.

In 1 Corinthians 9:5 Paul writes, *"Don't we have the right to take a believing wife along with us, as do the other Apostles and the Lord's brothers and Peter?"* The words "believing wife" in Greek is literally "sister wife." How could unmarried Paul speak of taking a "sister wife" along with him as he traveled, since we assume Paul had never married or that he was married earlier and his wife had died at an early age. Was he saying there were times when it was necessary for him to travel with a female missionary, giving the impression to strangers that they were married? This would enable the woman missionary to get from one place to another. Whether it happened to Paul we do not know, but his statement raises a question. Paul praises a number of important women in his letters, some of whom may have been traveling missionaries, like Paul. Was it necessary at times for them to travel together, and was this a practice followed by others in the early Church?

The disciples often exhibit an ample portion of human pride. Jesus caught them arguing among themselves about which of them was the greatest. His response was, *"Whoever wants to be first must be last of all and servant of all."* (Mark 9:35). In Luke's account of the same issue, Jesus said, *"Who is greater, the one who is at the table or the one who serves? Is it not the one who is at the table? But I am among you as one who serves."* (Luke 22:27 NRSV). At the last supper, Jesus was the one who served. In ancient and modern times, it is always the woman who serves, just like Jesus.

In Jesus' teaching and mode of life, there is a great reversal of values. More than once he says, "Many who are first will be last, and the last first." The disciples did not want mothers to bring their children to Jesus so he could bless them. Jesus rebuked the disciples: *"I tell you the truth, unless you change and become like little children, you will never enter the kingdom of heaven."* (Matt 18:3). This is another reversal when Jesus put the trust and receptivity of children as an example to the disciples. We may also include the parable of the rich man and Lazarus. In life, the rich man had it all, but in the life to come he lost it all and sick Lazarus had health and life. The parable of the day laborers in which those who only worked one hour are paid the same as those who worked all day, ends with "so the last will be first, and the first will be last." This is a reminder that those at the bottom in this life may be on top with God, both here and hereafter. In his life and ministry, Jesus honored and highlighted the role of women.

In both Matthew and Mark, there is the story of an unnamed woman who enters the home of Simon the Leper as Jesus is eating, and anoints his head with expensive ointment. Some of the disciples complained at what they felt to be a waste of money, which could have been given to the poor. Jesus defends the woman, saying she had anointed his body for burial beforehand. He added that what she did would be proclaimed everywhere in memory of her good deed. A remarkable tribute to a woman whose name we do not know. Untold numbers of women have made similar contributions to the well-being of the human family, and only God knows their names. "...The last shall be first."

There are three very similar stories of women who anoint Jesus as a sign of their appreciation for his obvious compassion. The first we have already looked at which took place in the home of Simon the Leper. It is also found in Mark 14:3ff. Another story is found in Luke 7:36, which took place in the home of a Pharisee. John's gospel has yet another story in John 12:1 which took place in the home of three siblings, Lazarus, Mary and Martha. During the meal, Mary anointed Jesus' feet with a very expensive perfume and wiped his feet with her hair. Some scholars believe that the story of the anointing was so popular that it was repeated in different settings as it was passed down through human memory before it was finally written. On the other hand, Jesus' obvious concern for women might have led to this expression of gratitude repeated more than once.

The movement to make women subordinate once again took place before the New Testament was completed. In 1 Timothy 2:11-15, which many scholars believe was not written by the Apostle Paul, but by one of his later followers, the author writes that women are to be submissive and modest, are not to be teachers of men. According to 1st Timothy, *"Adam was not the one deceived; it was the woman who was deceived and became a sinner."* (1 Tim 2:14). But is that really what happened according to the creation story? Go back to the third chapter of Genesis which records the "fall of man." It is true, Eve was the first to yield to the temptation to eat the forbidden fruit. She gave some of the fruit to Adam who ate it without objection or hesitation. When God confronted Adam over his disobedience, note Adam's defense: *"The woman you put here with me—she gave me some fruit from the tree, and I ate it."* (Gen 3:12). He was saying, "I had no choice except to eat it when that woman you put here with me gave me some to eat." Adam was indirectly blaming God who should never have created "that woman" in the first place. It makes us wonder how it could be possible that pastors and teachers can continue to promote the subordination of women based on the superiority of the man Adam. Some ultra conservative Protestant churches do not allow women to preach or teach or hold office in the church. The world's largest denomination does not allow women to be priests. Is that following Jesus?

There is a little bit of humor which probably should not be included here, but then, why not? We remember that every book in the Bible was written by men. With that in mind, the "story" goes that men later erased something from the Genesis account of the creation of the first man and first woman. The part erased was this: "God created the man first. Then, when God got good at it, God created woman."

The Apostle Paul apparently thought at least one woman was an apostle. In Romans 16:7 he wrote, "Greet Andronicus and Junia, my relatives who were in prison with me; they are prominent among the apostles, and they were in Christ before I was." Note that Paul calls both Andronicus and Junia apostles, and he says they were Christians before Paul was converted. In his letter to the Romans, Paul speaks of a woman whose name was Phoebe, who held the office of deacon, whom he strongly recommends, no doubt because of her considerable leadership ability: *"I commend to you our sister Phoebe, a deacon of the church at Cenchreae, so that you may welcome her in the Lord as is fitting for the saints, and help her in whatever she may require from you, for she has been a benefactor of many and of myself as well."* (Romans 16:1-2 NRSV). When Paul asks the Church in Rome to "welcome her in the Lord," was it because she was already on her way to Rome as a traveling missionary, like Paul? In chapter 16 of Romans the great apostle mentions at least nine women who were leaders in the church.

And yet, after about a hundred years, the church reverted to all male rule. At the Council of Nicaea in 325 CE, which was called and dominated by Emperor Constantine I, not one woman sat among the many handsomely robed male bishops. Did Peter deny Jesus again? Was this a forward step or a backward slide? Whatever it was, the absence of women did not come from Jesus. While we may be tempted to give thanks for the banquet which the emperor had with the bishops, we must never forget those happy meals Jesus had with the poor, the outcasts, prostitutes, sinners and women. Is the communal life of the church closer to the meals of Jesus or to the banquet of the emperor?

Chapter 14

CHRISTIANS AND MIRACLES

Jesus did not call on people simply to believe in miracles, but to perform miracles and to show superhuman power in their lives. Did not Jesus say, *"Ask and it will be given to you; seek and you will find; knock and the door will be opened to you."* (Matt 7:7).

The young man or woman who goes off to school and studies hard for years, believing that he or she can make a valuable contribution, and who discovers a new cure for an old illness has produced a miracle. And the man or woman who is living in the kingdom rule of God, daily embracing the way of Jesus, who cares deeply for his or her companion and children, who labors faithfully at their employment, contributing to the wellbeing of the human family, is also living miraculously. The miracle is in the expectation and the hard work. Anything is possible. There is no telling what the accepting and encouraging God might do in the life that is fully surrendered to the Heavenly Father, the God of Jesus.

We will never make that surrender until Jesus convinces us that his God can be fully trusted, who always encourages and never condemns. To make this surrender is what Jesus meant when he talked about entering the kingdom of God. The one who makes the surrender to the "Abba, Father" of Jesus is already living in the kingdom rule of God. Because the God of Jesus is for us and in us, we can live super lives.

The most important work of the church today is the rediscovery of Jesus in personal experience, but it must be the way the pre-crucifixion Christians experienced Him.

It is obvious that Jesus' main goal was people who were

missing the abundant life which he knew God wanted them to have. He regarded people as more important than anything else on earth and he thought that to lead them into a larger life of communion with God was earth's most important enterprise.

From the New Testament we learn that the abundant life consists in sins and guilt taken away, through rich communion with God in one's heart, aided and directed by the inner witness of God the Holy Spirit, and to know and follow Jesus Christ, who is the revelation of the ideal human and the God of limitless love.

Who would ever have imagined that a baby could be born in poverty, grow up in a carpenter's home, perhaps take up that trade when his father died, pursue God's call for a few months, would bless the lives of hundreds and then be murdered at age 33. He would organize no institutions, leave no writings and hold no position. He was driven by a compassionate heart which he experienced in God, he had a message for all people but he was especially drawn to the sick, the ignored, the confused and sinners. He was poor, and in his mission may have spent more nights sleeping on the ground than in a comfortable bed. For a while, he would be rejected by his own family who thought he was mentally ill, he would be branded as a heretic by his own religious leaders, and a traitor to his nation, and he would be crucified as one of the worst criminals. And yet, he is worshiped as Teacher, Friend, Savior and Lord 2000 years later. What could be more amazing?

The one thing that is more amazing is the experience of Jesus' followers soon after he died: they were certain he was still with them. The evidence for the resurrection is not the empty tomb, or the number of people who saw the resurrected Jesus; it is in people following the resurrection in every age, who have known from their experience that he was with them as they traveled through this world. A pastor may say to a hospital patient, "The Lord is with you," and invariably hear the response, "I know he is; I don't know what I would do without him." The Lord is with us now. The Lord is with you.

Chapter 15

WAS JESUS RIGHT?

The nagging question remains: was Jesus right about the unfailing love of God for all people? While Jesus experienced the love of the Father, his brutal death raises questions. The answer of many Christians also raises questions, when we believe that it was necessary for Jesus to die in order to placate the justice of God who required a sacrifice so great that no human being, nor all human beings past, present and future, could satisfy the demands of the holy and righteous God. This explanation insists that God must send his only son for the express purpose of dying a horrible death to satisfy God's holiness, thus purchasing forgiveness and eternal life in Heaven for all humans. But forgiveness and Heaven comes only if we are willing to believe that this whole scenario is true. And what does it say about a God who would make such demands?

While this thinking is accepted by many good Christians, it is a wholesale denial of Jesus' teaching about the love of God for all humans. It means that we must either disregard all that Jesus believed or rethink what we embrace about substitutionary theology. It is clear that the early church saw Jesus' death as serving a broader saving purpose. Paul says in Romans, *"Since all have sinned and fall short of the glory of God; they are now justified by his grace as a gift, through the redemption that is in Christ Jesus, whom God put forward as a sacrifice of atonement."* (Romans 3:23-25). In Galatians Paul says of Jesus, he *"gave himself for our sins to rescue us from the present evil age, according to the will of our God and Father."* (Gal 1:4).

Even if we conclude that Jesus was wrong in teaching that the love of God is extended to all people, what better way to live than to believe that the origin of the universe, this planet on which we reside, was conceived and brought forth by a Mystery which is compassionate and friendly, allowing for freedom and hope with the conviction that life is good and by God's grace extends into eternity.

But Jesus was not wrong. He lives on, vindicated by God through his resurrection. He is still testifying to the love of God for all, including the poor and the rich, the weak and the strong, the wise and the simple. He is for you and me. Praise God for Jesus. Praise God for God.

www.ingramcontent.com/pod-product-compliance
Lightning Source LLC
LaVergne TN
LVHW051639080426
835511LV00016B/2402